Making Your Money Work for You

How To Books are designed to help people achieve their goals. They are for everyone wishing to acquire new skills, develop self-reliance, or change their lives for the better. They are accessible, easy to read and easy to act on. Other titles in the series include:

Securing a Rewarding Retirement
How to really understand pensions and prepare successfully for your retirement

Saving and Investing
How to achieve financial security and make your money grow

Managing Your Personal Finances
How to achieve financial security and survive the shrinking welfare state

Dealing With Your Bank
How to assert yourself as a paying customer

Coping With Self Assessment
How to complete your tax return and minimise your tax bill

Investing in Stocks & Shares
A step-by-step handbook for the prudent investor

The *How To Series* now contains
around 250 titles in the following categories:

Business & Management
Computer Basics
General Reference
Jobs & Careers
Living & Working Abroad
Personal Finance
Self-Development
Small Business
Student Handbooks
Successful Writing

For full details, please send for a free copy of the latest catalogue to:
How To Books
Plymbridge House, Estover Road
Plymouth PL6 7PZ, United Kingdom
Tel: 01752 202301   Fax: 01752 202331
http://www.howtobooks.co.uk

Making Your Money Work for You

*How to use simple investment
principles to increase your wealth*

SIMON COLLINS

How To Books

First published in 1999 by
How To Books Ltd., 3 Newtec Place,
Magdalen Road, Oxford OX4 1RE, United Kingdom
Tel: 01865 793806   Fax: 01865 248780
email: info@howtobooks.co.uk
http://www.howtobooks.co.uk

British Library Cataloguing in Publication Data
A catalogue record for this book is available from
the British Library

Cartoons by Mike Flanagan
Editing by Julie Nelson
Cover design by Shireen Nathoo Design
Cover image PhotoDisc

Produced for How To Books by Deer Park Productions
Typeset by Euroset, Alresford, Hampshire SO24 9PQ
Printed and bound by The Cromwell Press, Trowbridge, Wiltshire.

NOTE: The material contained in this book is set out in good
faith for general guidance and no liability can be accepted
for loss or expense incurred as a result of relying in particular
circumstances on statements made in the book. The laws
and regulations are complex and liable to change, and readers
should check the current position with the relevant authorities
before making personal arrangements.

Contents

List of Illustrations

Preface

The world of investment is like a dark forbidding forest, with poorly marked paths that lead the wandering traveller from relatively open glades into gloom and silence. If you wish to pass that way, so the traditional wisdom goes, you should either take a guide with you or spend years studying the maps beforehand.

This book was inspired by the conviction that there is another way of looking at investment. There is no denying that it can be a very complicated business, but perhaps it is bound to be if you insist on trying to pick your way through by keeping your eyes to the ground. What if you could see over the top of all the trees, so you knew where you were at all times?

The chapters that follow explore three easy-to-use principles that you can use to manage your own wealth. We call them investment principles, but they aren't just about shares. Financial markets don't interest everyone, and your money won't all be in shares anyway. Even if you are thinking of buying property, paintings or cars, the principles work in the same way.

So long as you have the normal ration of common sense, putting your money to work is well within your powers. You do not need to be an expert, a mathematical genius, or even a compulsive reader of the *Financial Times*, although these people have their uses. When you can see where you're going, the forest is nothing to be frightened of.

Simon Collins

1

Clearing Your Mind

SORTING INCOME FROM WEALTH

Income and wealth are so often confused that you might be forgiven for thinking that they are the same thing. Even newspapers that ought to know better will explain that somebody is rich when they have an income of so much per year. It isn't necessarily true. 'Rich' is about wealth, and income may have nothing to do with it.

Getting straight about income and wealth is not being picky. It is part of the process of **clearing of your mind**. This sort of misunderstanding will make taking charge of your money more difficult than it needs to be.

Increasing your income is not the same as increasing your wealth. If you are looking for the former, you ought to think about changing your job, and you have bought the wrong book...

Getting it right

A good way of thinking about wealth is to imagine a fish tank with water in it (Figure 1). The higher the water level, the richer you are. This is

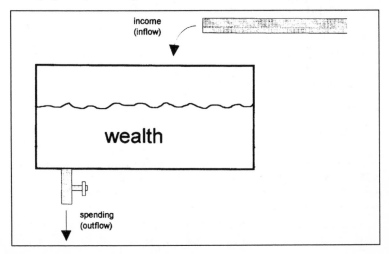

Fig. 1. The fish tank.

wealth. It is a **stock** of assets; it is what we apply 'rich' or 'poor' to, and **it is this quantity that we are seeking to manage**. Just what you want to manage it *for* is up to you.

The fish tank again

Imagine that the fish tank has a hose coming in at the top and a tap at the bottom. Any water coming into the tank via the hose is **income**, and any being drained from the bottom is **spending**. Income and spending are **flows**. They only affect wealth if the combined effect of water coming in and water coming out of the tank is a rise or fall in the overall water level.

If you have a high income, but spend it all, **your wealth will not grow**. This is why it is a mistake to assume that a footballer on a high salary is rich, for one thing does not imply the other.

Income and salary

Before we go any further, there is another distinction that you *must* understand. Income isn't only your wages, salary or pension. It may include 'one-off' gains from inheritance, selling your house at a higher price than you paid for it, or even winning the National Lottery! Often these forms of income will matter more to wealth than wages or salaries, because they tend to be relatively large and they are usually not spent all at once. They are like a big surge of water in the hose; the level in the tank rises sharply even if the tap at the bottom isn't completely shut.

ADDING UP RICHES

Before you can manage your wealth, you need to know what there is, and you need to know where it is going! It sounds like common sense, but getting down to it may not be so obvious. You will find it helpful to divide your wealth into two parts:

● **financial** wealth

● **non-financial** wealth

The first sort of wealth is what you own that has anything to do with the financial system: cash, bank accounts, shares and so on. This sort of wealth is what most people think of as 'money' and which they try to manage. But it is usually only part of the story!

As anyone unfortunate enough to have had a house fire will tell you, there is nothing like losing the lot for telling you just how much non-financial wealth you used to have. Leave aside thoughts of bank statements for a moment, and look about your own home. Making a list of all the possessions that you see would take quite some time, even if you consider your household a rather modest one.

Possessions are not always wealth, however. That fish tank would not normally include the light fittings, your shoes, or the wallpaper. It may be obvious that any jewellery or antique furniture would count as wealth, but between the diamond earrings and your wellies there must be some dividing line.

Drawing the line

Those possessions that are not wealth play no part in this book. If you can't decide whether something you own counts as wealth or not, ask yourself the following question. 'If I were to sell this possession, would the money I get for it justify a trip to the bank?'

In other words, if what you could get for it was not more than you would feel comfortable having in cash and in your pocket or purse, it isn't wealth. At least, it isn't wealth the way we mean it here.

This dividing line is undeniably a personal one. Some people are uncomfortable with more than £20 in cash in their pocket or purse, while others would be unconcerned if they had ten times as much. But this takes nothing away from the usefulness of the rule. Managing your money is a very personal matter too.

Spreading the net

Having taken a look at your possessions, and having decided what counts as wealth and what does not, you can turn to your financial wealth. These are usually far easier to reckon, since bank accounts, life insurance policies and the like all have numbers attached which are updated in regular statements. They should all be included within your wealth. Even **insurance policies linked to mortgages** and the **value of your house** even if it is mortgaged should be included. We shall see why below.

The list of items that count as your wealth is now reasonably comprehensive. Most, if not all, of what is in the fish tank is to be found under one of the headings. You may find it useful to refer back to this list when it comes to marking-to-market (see Chapter 2).

Rising or falling?

As we said right at the beginning, making your money work for you is a matter of managing your wealth. It only touches on income and spending when they affect your wealth. If we ignore any steps you may currently be taking to manage your wealth, we can say:

- If your income is higher than your spending, your wealth must be **increasing** (the level in that fish tank must be rising if more water flows in than flows out).

- If your spending is higher than your income, your wealth must be **decreasing**.

- If your spending is exactly the same as your income, your wealth is **not changing**.

It follows from all this that keeping tabs on what flows in and what flows out is essential to managing your wealth. It is surprising just how much advice on the subject avoids this very basic matter. Income and spending have a direct effect on how your wealth is changing.

What is the point of running off to buy shares if you don't even know whether your wealth is rising or falling (and by how much)? It would be like setting off into the desert without checking your water-bottle.

MEASURING YOUR INCOME

Knowing what is flowing into that fish tank sounds too easy to be true. Which is probably why mistakes happen. For it isn't simply a matter of saying, 'Well, I know what I'm paid'. As pointed out above, wages or salary isn't necessarily all there is to your income. Even if it were, you probably have taxes to pay, and tax rates do change. Keep up to date.

Income is income
Any irregular income flows – bonuses from work or from investments, unexpected gifts and so on – are not 'spending'! Avoid the temptation to earmark them for special treats and therefore dispense with recording them. Nobody is saying you can't buy what you wish with it, but you should note it as income nonetheless. The sooner you can see that your spending comes out of your wealth and your income adds to your wealth, the sooner you are going to master your affairs. You can't have income that 'doesn't count', just as you can't have spending that 'doesn't count'. It *all* counts!

TRACKING YOUR SPENDING

The 'outflow' at the bottom of that fish tank is usually a little more complicated to quantify than income. While the sources of our income are limited – usually our pay or pension plus the odd irregular item – we spend our money in hundreds of different ways and in dozens of shops every single month.

There *are* people who carefully note every item of expenditure in a little book. It's probably something we've all tried at least once. It's one thing to keep track of the major items and quite another to jot absolutely everything down. It takes a rather special kind of mind that can patiently sit down every night and faithfully record every purchase of the day, from the newspaper to the half-a-dozen apples picked up at the market stall outside the station.

The problem is that if you don't know what you're spending, you don't know what is happening to your wealth. You really *do* need to know how much is going on newspapers and the thousand and one other bits and pieces because they all add up sooner or later! Fortunately, you can get around having to scratch away in a notebook all night.

Dealing with cash

Reckoning up what you have spent by writing cheques presents no problem at all, even if you want to check up without waiting for a statement to arrive from your bank. As long as you fill in your stubs (it only takes a second or two!) it's right there in front of you. Items you purchase with a credit or switch card are marked on receipts. But the things you can't track are usually too small individually to justify writing a cheque or producing a credit card, and half the time there's no receipt either.

The short cut consists of simply treating any cash you withdraw from the bank as being spent *the moment you draw it.* So long as you ask for a receipt from the cash machine, nothing needs to get written down. You needn't change anything else you currently do. When it comes to counting up what you've spent, *ignore* whatever unspent cash remains in your pocket or purse. It's already accounted for.

Current spending and investment

Spending has another complication which income does not have. It's all very well counting up all my spending, you may say, but some of my spending is on investments of one sort or another! It's not strictly true that all spending is pouring out of the bottom of that tank! If I go out and buy something that I would count as wealth according to the definition in 'Adding up Riches' above, it doesn't flow out at all! It stays right there, in the tank!

This is why you need to distinguish between two forms of spending. When you come to reckon up what you have spent, you need to separate what we can call **current spending** from **investment**:

- **Current spending** may add to your possessions, but it does *not* add to your wealth. You either use it up (e.g. food and drink, cinema tickets) or it adds to your pile of possessions without being worth enough to be wealth (see that defining line in 'Adding up Riches').

- **Investmen**t is what you *can* count as wealth. You don't use it up and you can sell it for more cash than you would wish to carry about with you.

Investment needs to be noted, of course, but when it comes to working out what you have spent in a given month, include only current spending. Investment is taken into account separately, as we see in Chapter 2.

Running a routine

Because spending is more difficult to keep track of than income, you may care to keep abreast of your spending on a regular and frequent basis. Every week or two – and at least once a month – you could sit down and run through the following steps:

1. Jot the headings 'current' and 'investment' on a piece of paper.

2. Go through your chequebook stubs, and write the amount of each cheque under either of the two headings. Mark each stub (with a tick, say) so you don't count it all over again next time.

3. Pull out all your credit card and switch card receipts from wherever you keep them, and go through the same procedure. When you have noted the amount, either throw the receipts away or, if you prefer to keep them to check your statement or for guarantee purposes, file them.

4. Follow the same procedure for receipts of cash withdrawals from teller machines. These amounts will almost always be current spending items. (If you bought something that counts as wealth with cash, you will remember it anyway.) *Ignore* any cash you have in your pocket, purse or wallet.

5. Add up the two columns. The current spending total is what is flowing out of the tank. If your income is *less* than this figure, your wealth (ignoring what your investments may have gained) is shrinking.

TAKING LOANS INTO ACCOUNT

All that you borrow and all that you lend needs to be taken into account when assessing your wealth:

● What you **borrow** – including a mortgage on your house – reduces your wealth. In the case of a mortgage, you have already taken the value of the house and any associated insurance policies into account in reckoning wealth, so it is only fair that you count the whole of the mortgage against them.

● What you **lend** should be included within your wealth, even if there is no specific date for repayment (e.g. a loan to a friend or relative). If it is not really intended to be repaid at all (e.g. a loan to one of your children) it isn't really a loan and it should be forgotten about altogether. Leave it out of your calculations. If it does happen to get repaid, treat it as windfall income (see 'Measuring your Income' above).

If you are paying interest on a loan, the regular payments should be included in your current spending. If you receive interest on loans you make to other people, that gets counted as income.

STAKING THE BOUNDARIES

This chapter is about laying the foundations for successful management of your money. There are definitions to take on board, then a 'stocktake' of what wealth you have (the contents of the fish tank) and what you have coming in and going out (inflows and outflows). Before we continue, however, one possible worry needs to be dealt with.

Things not available for management
When you added up your wealth, you will have included items (usually non-financial) that you have no intention of 'managing'. You may feel some apprehension about exposing them to the harsh glare of investment principles! You may have inherited or been given things that not only have money value but also have sentimental value. **Cross these items off the list!**

If thinking about their money value encourages you to get them properly insured, that is all to the good. But as far as this book is concerned, these items are staked off from wealth available for management and will *not* be included in our discussion from now on. Sentimental value cannot be measured, and we won't even try!

MAKING RECORDING A HABIT

There has already been mention of making lists, writing things down and so on. The need to keep clear records is going to grow rather than diminish as you take charge of your money.

● **Use one of the following:**
  – a robust, large-format notebook
  – a computer spreadsheet.

● **Do not rely on:**
  – loose leaves of paper
  – small pocket-books
  – your memory.

As far as computers are concerned, don't worry if you don't have one. People have been keeping clear and accurate records of their finances since ancient times, after all. And there's no denying the aesthetic advantage of well-kept books over computer screens! But if you have a computer, you will know how useful they can be (remember to back up your files!). The choice is yours.

Starting it off

If you haven't started already, now would be a good point to set down all the information touched on so far. The following steps are also illustrated in Figure 2:

1. List all the items that you count as wealth financial *and* non-financial ('Adding up Riches', above). Don't worry if you don't have precise numbers for their value – we come to that in Chapter 2.

2. Note your current income. This means income you have or will receive **this month**.

3. If you haven't yet started to track your spending, start doing so now. If you do it on a monthly basis you make it easy to compare it with your income. Don't forget to distinguish between **current spending** and **investment**. Any spending of the second type should be added to your list of wealth items.

4. Adjust your wealth for loans.

5. Remove items from your wealth list that you are unlikely ever to sell and do not wish to 'manage'.

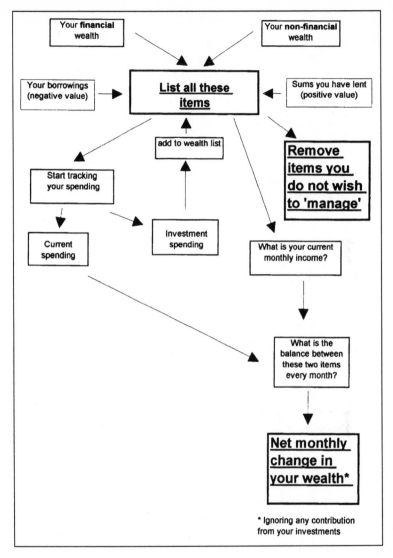

Fig. 2. Starting your records.

SUMMARY

1. Income is not wealth.

2. Wealth is a **stock** of income, and spending are **flows** into and out of it.

3. If your spending rises with your income, your wealth will not increase.

4. Your wealth may include non-financial as well as financial items.

5. To decide whether any of your non-financial possessions count as wealth, ask yourself the following: 'If I were to sell this possession, would the money I get for it justify a trip to the bank?'

6. You cannot begin to make your money work for you unless you track both your income and your spending.

7. Track your spending using the five-step process described in 'Running a routine' above.

8. Adjust your wealth for any loans you have made or taken out, **including mortgages**.

9. Remove wealth items that you do not wish to include in any form of management (those with significant sentimental value). They will not count from now on.

10. Keep clear and accurate records of your wealth, income and spending, either in a large-format notebook or on a computer spreadsheet.

POINTS TO CONSIDER

1. If you are conscientiously recording your income and spending, how would you treat a cash gift? If cash should count as spending as soon as you have it in your pocket or purse, how can it be accounted for?

2. If you own a house and still have an outstanding mortgage, have you ever sat down and worked out whether you could use any of your wealth to reduce that mortgage? If you have a deposit or savings account that you haven't touched for years and are unlikely to need to tap in the foreseeable future, have you ever compared the interest you receive on it with the interest you pay on the same amount of a mortgage, even including tax considerations?

3. Are you truly wealthy if your sole possessions of value are three Rembrandt portraits that you would never sell?

2

Taking Charge of Your Wealth

MARKING-TO-MARKET

Marking-to-market is an *essential* component of successful money management. The term is widely used among professionals, fund managers and traders in financial markets. Using it yourself for managing your own money is not pretension, however. Look at it as a perpetual reminder of how seriously you intend to take the whole matter.

Staying on top

In Chapter 1 you listed all the components of your wealth, both financial and non-financial. There were some things on that list (almost certainly in the non-financial part) that you would not care to put a money value on, for sentimental or similar reasons. And we excluded these items from that part of your wealth that is available to be managed. But for all that remains you should attribute definite values, that is, pounds and pence.

This is what **marking-to-market** is all about. It is simply the process of 'marking' every component of the wealth that you propose to manage with a 'market' price. This need not be any more complicated than writing a number of pounds after every item on your list. And it applies to your house or golf club membership just as much as it does to any shares you own.

This exercise needs to be repeated on a regular basis. Once a month would be appropriate. The mark-to-market is essential for the following reasons:

● It brings to your notice any unusual rise or fall in the value of something you own.

● Being up to date *always* improves the quality of your decision-making.

● It forces you to remain objective about your investments. You control them, not the other way around.

Doing the books

Whether you mark-to-market by writing in a notebook or using a computer spreadsheet, tracking the value of your wealth needs to be a careful exercise. Every bit as careful, in fact, as that of any self-respecting Victorian housekeeper. Thus there should not be entries such as the following:

● 'value roughly' so-and-so

● 'assume same as last valuation'

● 'no time to check'.

Sloppiness, in other words, is out. It is absolutely no good you trying to take charge of your money if you can't be bothered to track what you have.

Financial and non-financial

The distinction between these two types of wealth was made in Chapter 1. You may find it helpful to separate them in your mark-to-market exercise, since financial wealth items (**financial assets**, if you prefer) tend to change price much more readily than non-financial items (**non-financial assets**). You will probably find they require more active management, too.

Pricing the priceless

If you have financial wealth (e.g. shares, bonds, unit trusts, bank deposits), updating their values in your regular mark-to-market is straightforward. Their values will normally appear in the financial press. Buying a *Financial Times* on the day you appoint to go over your books would normally be all that you would require. Some financial assets need less effort still. You receive regular statements of your bank balance, for example.

Non-financial wealth items are not usually as easy. Nonetheless, finding up to date values for them is just as important. If you own a house, for instance, it would be excessive to get estate agents to value it every month. But a careful look at the windows of estate agents every month ought to give you a good feel for what your house is worth. Obviously, you won't get a value down to the nearest pound, but a calculated estimate is infinitely better than a baseless guess.

In all cases, financial and non-financial, bear in mind that **the price at which you ought to value something is not necessarily the same thing as the price of a new or identical one**. This is a point that we will examine more closely in Chapter 5. For the moment, you should take great care in attributing values of what you own on the basis of *where you believe you can sell them*, not where you can buy more of the same.

MANAGING DEPRECIATION

If you own a car, you will know that this particular asset typically falls in value over its lifetime. It is true that some cars become 'classics', and their value may rise over time, but very few of us own such a vehicle. We buy a new or second-hand machine in the expectation that we will eventually sell it for much less than we paid for it.

Appreciation and depreciation

Assets that rise in value are called 'appreciating' ones, and those that lose value – like cars – are described as 'depreciating'. These are terms that you will come across time and again in investment matters.

It may have occurred to you that managing your money is not as simple as trying to make your assets worth more all the time. If this were so, you would never buy a modern car. Your willingness to hold a depreciating asset may well be understandable, for it gets you to work, or it is a necessary part of the way you live. But it doesn't change the fact that managing your money is as often about **controlling depreciation** as it is about making it grow.

Depreciating in practice

If you are a car owner, did you give any thought to depreciation when you bought it? You may have referred to resale or second-hand value, which in this case comes to the same thing. You may have preferred one car over another similarly priced one precisely because its value was expected to 'hold up' better. This is what controlling depreciation is all about.

When you sit down every so often to perform your mark-to-market, the same applies to cars as it does to shares or houses. You should make a point of making a good estimate of the resale value of your car, and enter that along with everything else. For most common makes, such information is readily available from your newsagents: *Exchange & Mart*, *Auto Trader* and several other publications of this type are perfect for the job. Once again, **beware of the values listed** – they may be purchase or 'trade' prices rather than where *you* can sell. You may need to adjust quoted figures downwards for your own mark-to-market purposes.

Cars are not the only depreciating asset, though they are by far the most common. You may wish to hold certain financial assets that are falling in value, to take a different example, because you believe that they may well climb rapidly in the future. In that case, too, the same principles of marking-to-market apply. Depreciating assets need to be watched every bit as carefully as the appreciating kind.

REGARDING THE FUTURE

The mark-to-market is essential. but it is not the only necessary preparation for managing your money. Alongside the technical business of valuing all that you propose to manage, you must give thought to any future commitments for which you will have to provide. This will colour your attitude to much of what you decide to do.

Listing commitments

If your future commitments have a price and a date on them, so much the better. Unfortunately, life is rarely so simple and there will often be 'unknowns'. Keeping a list and updating it when you feel the need is still most worthwhile. The sorts of things that we're talking about would include the following:

- **Price and date known:**
  - imminent holidays
  - purchase of new car.

- **Price or date known:**
  - school fees for children
  - extension or renovation of house
  - major celebration (anniversary, retirement, etc.).

- **Neither price nor date known:**
  - marriage of children
  - care of elderly relative.
  - purchase of second home.

You might consider revisiting your list of future commitments as often as you mark-to-market. And like the mark-to-market, it needs to be brought up to date regularly. New commitments may turn up, others may disappear, and yet others may become clearer. The point of the exercise, however, is not simply keeping everything neat and tidy, useful though that is. **It is to prevent you making inappropriate investment decisions when the time comes**, especially with respect to maturity (Chapters 3 and 4).

Adjusting for uncertainty

It may be that you are particularly cautious, and wish to keep part of your wealth in a readily available form – in a current account, say, or even under the mattress. You may wish to have funds readily available to provide for some undefined future event, 'because you never know'.

Even if the need is undefined in this case, you should include it on your list of future commitments. Decide the amount you wish to keep readily available, and list the item *as if* it is required within the next week or month. And reinsert it each time you update that list. There is no reason why even this sum should be left unaccounted for, and never reconsidered.

SETTING YOUR OBJECTIVES

The whole exercise of managing your own money needs to have at least one **objective**. Objectives have three functions:

1. They remind you of why you are making the effort.

2. They measure how successful you are.

3. They guide your decision-making.

Spending a little time in serious thought about your objectives avoids a lot of muddled thinking later on. The interesting thing about it is that you may well find that your reasons for managing your money are not as obvious as you first thought. Making your wealth grow, for example, is usually only part of it. You may find that a desire for greater control over your affairs is at least as important, or that you wish to invest in certain assets that matter to you – even if they are not the most profitable.

Making the effort

It is one thing to be enthusiastic at the outset, while you take your money from the hands of banks and fund managers and place it here and there on your own say-so. It is quite another when it is all invested, and there is nothing to do for several months save your regular marking-to-market exercises. There may also be times when you find it difficult to decide where to invest your money, or when particular investments are not doing as well as you had hoped. At times like these you may find yourself wishing that you'd left it all to 'the experts'.

Knowing what you are doing it all for gives you courage! Having a reminder before you at tedious or difficult times puts the immediate problem into a wider (and hopefully happier) perspective. It's a bit like redecorating. Being 'stuck' on a fiddly corner of the room is a lot easier to bear if you can think of what the end result is going to be.

Measuring success

An objective also enables you to judge your own efforts. You need to know how well your management of your money is working. Merely saying, 'Well, it'll be obvious' just won't do. For it *isn't* always obvious. What may happen is that you start off saying that you want to increase your wealth by more than bank deposits would return each year, but if this proves difficult you may convince yourself that you wanted to keep it as safe as bank deposits instead. It is this kind of drifting that you should avoid.

In the end, you need to be able to make some sort of objective judgement. You need to be able to say whether you are meeting your objectives or not. If you are, you can take comfort from the fact that you are doing a good job and that you should keep at it. If you are persistently falling short of your objectives, then you know that all is not well, either with you or with the objectives themselves.

Aiding your decisions

There will be many occasions when you are tempted to invest in something you've just read about, or which a professional expert has to offer. Even the most cautious of us have been known to jump at a good idea if it is presented in the right way. Knowing your objectives can act as a shield against over-hasty decisions, and prevent you straying off into places you never intended to visit.

It could be that one of your objectives is to keep your investments out of industrial activities that you feel are morally doubtful. Many people would prefer not to invest in armaments or tobacco, for example. Or perhaps there are certain countries you would rather not be involved with, either for political reasons or because you consider them too risky. Whatever your preferences, **a stated objective will force you to look into any investment opportunity with greater thoroughness than would otherwise be the case**.

Securing your happiness

Look at your objectives as **guiding principles** of your money management. Some objectives may have already occurred to you, but if they haven't, or if you're not sure whether you ought to add some more, some suggestions follow. You will note that some are positive (i.e. targets for what you want to achieve), and others are negative in character (i.e. restrictions you wish to impose on yourself):

- 'I wish to increase my total asset value every year by at least the rate of inflation.'

- 'So long as house prices rise, I need only maintain the current value of my financial assets.'

- 'I do not want any exposure to the Japanese economy.'

- 'I want no more than half of my financial assets held as shares.'

- 'The only financial assets I wish to buy are those which I can be sure of selling easily.'

- 'I wish at least part of my investments to support businesses based in my home region.'

It should be emphasised that the objectives you set need to be genuinely yours. If you take them from this book or anywhere else simply because they sound sensible, the chances are that you won't take them seriously enough when they could really help you.

LIMITING YOUR RISKS

Financial and non-financial assets alike carry **risk**. As sages have remarked down through the ages, there is absolutely nothing on earth or even in the skies that cannot and will not change. There cannot be any investment that is 100 per cent safe. Try and think of one. Can you not imagine anything *at all* that might make it worthless?

A common-sense scale
However you put your money to work, it can never be as straightforward as investing one part in 'safe' assets and another in 'risky' ones. Since all assets are risky to some extent, it is better to think of all investment possibilities as lying along a scale that has 'as safe as possible' at one end and 'extremely risky' at the other.

Calling some of your assets 'rock solid' or something of that sort is not helpful to money management. It may stop you monitoring their condition, and in the worst case, you may be so blinded by the notion that you fail to notice something going seriously wrong – until it is all too late.

Agreeing the rule-book

If the objectives that you have set yourself (see previous section) do not include any consideration of the risks you are prepared to take and those you are not, pay attention to that now. You will find it most helpful to your future investment decisions if you have set your **risk limits**.

Such limits do not require that you analyse every possible investment and list those that you would rather not touch. It can be much simpler than that. Consider the following examples:

- 'I will not deposit any money with a bank outside the UK 'big four' (Lloyds-TSB, HSBC Midland, NatWest, Barclays) unless I have checked its quality first with someone I trust.'

- 'I will not invest in non-financial assets that are known to change price rapidly.'

- 'I will not place more than one-third of my financial assets in a single investment.'

- 'I will try as far as possible to avoid putting my principal at risk when I invest.'

Getting involved in investments that carry more risk than you really want is almost always a gradual process. It won't happen if you keep to your own rules.

WRITING IT DOWN

As in Chapter 1, you have been advised to write things down several times. Whether 'writing' means handwritten entries in a notebook or material stored on a personal computer, there are four new elements:

1. All marking-to-market of wealth available to be managed.

2. A list of your future financial commitments.

3. A list of your objectives in managing your own money.

4. Your risk limits, if not already included in 'objectives'.

Having your decisions to hand

Whenever you are making decisions about your money, or listening to advice, have your objectives and risk limits to hand. They will act just like a racehorse's blinkers – and allow you to concentrate on what *you* want to do without distractions. There are many forms of financial and non-financial investment out there that sound great but which are not right for you. Having your rules and situation before you will save a great deal of your time and effort – and possibly your money.

SUMMARY

1. Regular 'marking-to-market' of assets available to be managed is essential.

2. The marking-to-market exercise should be serious and as precise as possible, not rough-and-ready.

3. The appropriate prices to use for your mark-to-market should be those where you think you can sell your assets, not where you can buy more of the same. There is usually a difference between the two.

4. Good money management has as much to do with controlling depreciation as it does with encouraging appreciation.

5. Listing future financial commitments – even if all details are not yet known – will prove invaluable when making decisions about investment maturities.

6. You should set objectives for managing your own money. Some could be in the form of targets, and others could remind you to steer clear of particular investments.

7. There is no such thing as a totally risk-free investment, but some are clearly safer than others.

8. Set risk limits or risk rules for yourself, based on what you consider to be sensible. They will prevent you being tempted by investments that do not suit you.

9. You should record your mark-to-market, future commitments, objectives and risk rules.

10. You should have your objectives and risk rules before you when making investment decisions or listening to advice.

POINTS TO CONSIDER

1. What would you think of neighbours who were going to buy a new car but went round to a local car-hire firm and hired the same model week after week for a year? If the weekly hire charge were £130,

would you consider them mad? Are they madder than you if you go out and buy the same car for £15,000, expecting it to be worth only £8,000 in a year's time?

2. If you count your house as a non-financial wealth item that needs to be managed with your financial wealth, do you follow your local property market? If you follow your shares to the nearest penny, why leave your house's value to guesswork?

3. If there were no speed limits on the roads, would you always stick to a safe speed? Would it guarantee that you would never be involved in an accident? Does this tell you anything about setting risk limits?

3

Creating a Portfolio

THINKING OBJECTIVELY

One of the lesser-known secrets of successful investment is being objective. Surprisingly, becoming attached to strategies that are not working is a disease by no means confined to the amateur! Professionals on the world's financial markets and others that advise on non-financial investments (e.g. the housing market) are sometimes extremely slow to give up their cherished ideas.

Emotional attachments

So far you have identified what wealth you have, put a value on it, and calculated how it changes every passing month with your income and spending. You have numbers before you, and the more you concentrate on the numbers rather than what lies behind them the better you will be at investing and managing your wealth in general.

Don't get emotionally involved! If you feel unhappy about treating any asset purely as a number, it shouldn't be sitting there in your mark-to-market. It should have been excluded from the start as something of sentimental value (see Chapter 1, 'Staking the Boundaries'). In principle, you should be prepared to sell or reduce all the financial and non-financial assets that you have listed as available to be managed.

Living up to the ideal

Describing the collection of financial and non-financial assets that you will manage is part of getting clinical about the whole thing. There are other advantages too:

- It reinforces the notion that your wealth, whether financial or non-financial, can be managed *as a unit,* with one set of rules.

- It stops you treating any one part of your wealth (e.g. a sum in a bank deposit account) as something independent of everything else.

LOOKING AT IT THREE WAYS

Your wealth – we can call it your **portfolio** – may be analysed from three different directions (Figure 3):

1. maturity

2. expected return

3. risk.

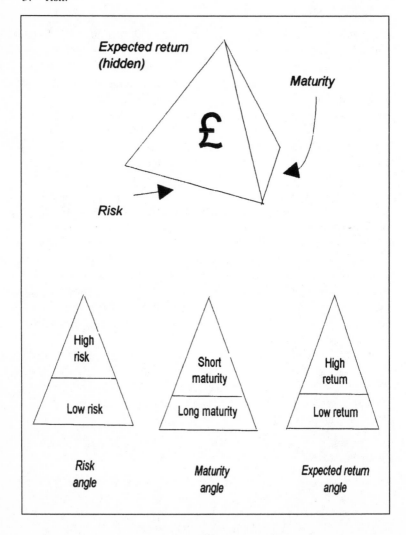

Fig. 3. Your wealth from three angles.

Every time you make an investment decision, you will affect the look of your portfolio from at least one of these three angles. Thus every investment, financial or non-financial, can be analysed on its own in terms of these three elements. You shouldn't be buying *anything* without giving some consideration to each.

These are the **investment principles** referred to in the Preface. Each of them has two merits:

1. They allow you to compare the potential investment or your portfolio with any objectives you have set yourself (Chapter 2).

2. They enable you to make rational comparisons between different investments.

We take a brief look at all three below, returning to them in some detail in the chapters that follow.

DEFINING MATURITIES

From now on, every investment you make should have a **maturity** attached to it. This is the length of time you are planning to hold the asset. Think of it as the **term** of your investment, if you prefer.

Many financial investments have maturities already specified. They 'expire' after a certain time, whether you like it or not. If you put your money in a three-year National Savings bond, for example, you would say that this investment has a three-year maturity. When this period has elapsed you will no longer have a savings bond but your initial investment plus interest in cash or as a cheque.

Dealing with unknowns

There is a problem, of course, with investments that do not come with an 'expiry date' attached. It is not necessarily evident why all investments need a maturity of any sort, and in any case the maturity of an investment in a house, an ordinary deposit account or a car is not so clear.

All investments that count as wealth to be managed need a maturity:

● You are not managing your money *at all* if you invest without any idea of how long you plan to hold the asset!

● For any given maturity there will be a range of different assets to choose from. By refusing to give an asset a maturity, you may be denying yourself the benefit of a more suitable investment.

● As we shall see, it makes good sense to match your investments with the future commitments discussed in Chapter 2. Assigning maturities to investments makes this process much easier.

Assets that do not have maturities 'attached' require you to provide them. This applies whether we are talking of a house, a share purchase or a new car. Ask yourself, 'Just how long do I plan to hold this asset?' If the investment is genuinely long-term (*is* it?), apply a **long-term** maturity (5, 10 or even 20 years) to it. On the other end of the scale, a current account at the bank might be regarded as a very **short-term** investment. You might even assign a one-month maturity to it, since your balance on the account may vary considerably over that time.

Maturity profile

If all your assets have maturities, we may describe **the maturity profile** of your entire portfolio. This means that we may say, for example, that one-quarter of your wealth is invested in assets that mature in less than a year, one-quarter in assets that mature between one and five years, and the rest in assets that mature between five and twenty years.

This profile will change as assets mature and you make new investment decisions. At any one point, however, this 'snapshot' of what your wealth looks like may prove invaluable:

● It will tell you if you are straying from any general maturity guidelines you have set yourself (see Chapter 1).

● If your portfolio looks unbalanced (i.e. too much wealth in a particular maturity range, in your opinion), it will direct which maturity you choose for the next investment you make.

INTRODUCING EXPECTED RETURN

Like maturity, expected return has a detailed chapter all of its own (Chapter 6). It is certainly the most mathematical way of looking at your portfolio or any single investment, and may therefore require particular attention.

Unfortunately, mathematics can't be left out of investment decisions altogether! After all, you attached numbers to your assets, your income and your spending in order to make sense of them, and it would be a bit much to expect them to leave the party so early.

Getting used to the idea

Every investment you make has a **return** when it arrives at its maturity date. The return is either positive (the investment gains value), negative (the investment loses value), or, conceivably, zero (it neither gains nor loses value). Your regular mark-to-market will tell you what that return is looking like at any one time.

Return on its own is pretty useless as an investment principle. When you invest your money, you are more interested in what that investment will be worth in the future than in how it performed in the past. This is why we use **expected return** as a principle instead.

Expected return is simply a calculated guess about what the return on any given investment (or, by extension, the portfolio as a whole) will be. As this guess is expressed in numbers, this is where the maths comes in.

We go into the detail later. The important thing for now is to realise that the 'calculated guess' is going to be *your* calculated guess. If this sounds daunting ('I don't know *anything* about investments, let alone guess what they will be worth!'), take heart. As we shall see, there's not much to it that simple common sense and your own experience of life doesn't cover.

HEDGING YOUR BETS

As anyone familiar with the Turf will tell you, you hedge your bets in order to limit **risk**. The downside of such an operation, of course, is that you give up some of the 'win' if you turn out to be right. This is effectively what you are doing when you decide to invest in a number of different assets. You have almost certainly hedged some of your bets already: you have financial as well as non-financial assets, for a start.

As a general rule, **the wider the range of your investments, the less spectacular the gains and losses on your portfolio**. Whether this is good or bad depends on your point of view, but take a moment to think about it. In Chapter 2 you set your own risk limits. In the light of this general rule, do your risk rules need any modification?

Risk and reward

It will be no surprise to you to learn that high-return investments (those with the highest expected return) are often the riskiest. 'What's the catch?' is a perfectly natural and sensible reaction to investments that look especially good.

There are not many bargains out there, for either financial or non-financial investments. Certainly very few that you should make an unconsidered grab for. While you would probably be too cautious if you were to say that any investment with a return above such-and-such a level is too risky for you, be aware that nobody is going to give you a high return for free. The price you pay is almost always higher risk.

Keeping to favourites

From a risk point of view, there is great comfort in investing your money in assets that are familiar to you. Your house will be there tomorrow, you tell yourself, and British Telecom is not going to go into liquidation any time soon. Furthermore, you will know what property prices ought to be in your area, and you can see what BT shares are worth from a quick glance at the newspaper. Neither is going to change very much without you knowing about it. So why bother with anything you don't follow or haven't even heard of?

There is nothing wrong with keeping your money in investments with which you are comfortable. You might note the following points, however:

● If an investment is well-known to you it doesn't always mean that it can't be relatively risky.

● If you shut your mind to unfamiliar forms of investment, you are almost certainly shutting yourself off from much that is just as safe and worthwhile.

Prudence in learning

It is not recklessness if you set about learning about investment opportunities that are new to you. Quite the opposite, in fact! Your natural bias in favour of the tried and tested comes from your impression that what you know must also be safe. But why should that necessarily follow?

Prudent money management doesn't have to mean popping it all in your local building society. Think of it instead as including a rational analysis of all forms of investment, familiar or not.

Staying at home or going abroad?

British investments are not necessarily the safest in themselves. Why should they be? You probably know of American, German or other European investments that must be at least as safe. It is hard to distinguish between shares in British Airways and shares in KLM as far as risk is concerned.

The problem – adding to your risk

Putting your money in bank deposits abroad (e.g. in euro deposits) or in the shares of foreign companies can create additional risk. This risk has nothing to do with how safe the bank or company is in itself. Professionals sometimes call it **translation risk** – it is the risk that any gains on your investment may be lost by changes in the value of the pound against other currencies.

A worked example
Assume that you feel that a bank deposit held in Germany is about as safe as a bank deposit can possibly be. You can see from a copy of the *Financial Times* that the interest paid on such a deposit would not be generous, but you feel that the relative safety of your money is more important than a high return.

Assume further that you have **£10,000** to deposit, and you exchange it for euros at the rate of £1 = 1.4 euros. Assume you place these euros on deposit for one year in Germany, at an agreed return of 3 per cent.

At the end of this one year, you will have 14,000 euros (the original equivalent of £10,000) plus 420 euros (interest), or a total of **14,420 euros**. So far, no extra risk. The **translation risk** comes in **if you decide to turn your euros back into pounds**. For exchange rates are constantly moving. If the £:euro exchange rate after your one year is not £1 = 1.4 euros, but (for example) £1 = 1.5 euros, then your 14,420 euros are worth a little over **£9,600** (14,420 divided by 1.5 equals 9613.33). You will have **lost** money, despite the secure nature of your investment!

Investing abroad: the point to remember
What the above shows is that if you invest your money abroad, you are adding a new risk – that of currencies changing value – to the risk of the investment itself. It may be, of course, that you gain rather than lose as currencies fluctuate. **But remember that this risk exists no matter how safe the foreign investment is in itself.**

BALANCING YOUR ASSESSMENT

Whether you use a computer or pen and paper, you should get into the habit of assessing your portfolio and possible future investments in a methodical fashion. This means looking at the portfolio or investment in the light of each investment principle in turn, giving you a balanced assessment.

Preparing the ground
Of the three investment principles – maturity, expected return and risk –

the first two make for easy comparisons and allow you to rank investments easily:

● Since you give every asset you own or propose to buy a **maturity**, there is not much to this part. Either a proposed investment fits into the maturity profile you want, or it doesn't. If you are looking for a one-year investment, for example, shares may be for you (you can sell them as easily within one year as you can in five), but property is probably inappropriate.

● **Expected return**, as we shall see, is expressed as a number. Three potential investments with the same maturity will almost certainly have different expected returns. The higher the expected return, the more tempting the investment would be.

● **Risk** doesn't always come with numbers attached, although there is nothing stopping you classifying risks by number. It is probably easier to define the riskiness of an investment in a more general fashion. Why not classify potential investments as 'low risk', 'reasonable risk', 'high risk' and 'too risky'? Your judgement, is of course, crucial in making these distinctions. Which is as it should be.

If you can keep tabs on your portfolio by breaking it down by each of the criteria, so much the better. A **balanced portfolio** has a range of maturities, expected returns and risks, as shown in Figure 4.

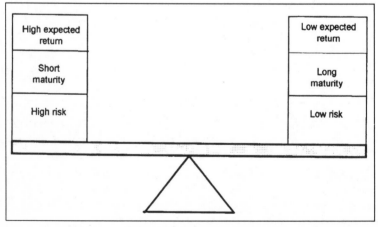

Fig. 4. A balanced portfolio.

SUMMARY

1. Force yourself to be as objective as possible about your potential investments. If sentiment is involved, this book cannot help you.

2. We call the sum total of all your financial and non-financial assets **your portfolio**. Like any individual investment, it may be assessed with investment principles.

3. The three investment principles are **maturity**, **expected return** and **risk**. Each represents a different way of looking at an investment or your portfolio.

4. You should attach a maturity to every investment you make. If it doesn't come with a specific 'expiry date' (property, for example), assign one to it.

5. If all your assets have maturities, we may describe **the maturity profile** of your entire portfolio. This profile will change as assets mature and you make new investment decisions.

6. Expected return is *your* calculated guess about what the return on any given investment – or, by extension, the portfolio as a whole – will be. Expected return is expressed as a number.

7. As a general rule, **the wider the range of your investments, the less spectacular the gains and losses on your portfolio**. Whether this is good or bad depends on your point of view, but you must bear it in mind.

8. High-return investments (those with the highest expected return) are often the riskiest. Ask yourself, 'What's the catch?'

9. While most risk considerations apply to any investment, investing abroad incurs an additional risk connected with exchange rate movements. This is called **translation risk**.

10. Assess your portfolio and possible investments in the light of each investment principle in turn. This will give you a balanced assessment.

POINTS TO CONSIDER

1. Why do stock markets and property prices occasionally 'crash'? Do you think that the bad news that triggers them bursts onto the scene all at once? Why do people not react to bad news until it is too late?

2. Why would an investment adviser show *you* the bargain of the century?

3. If the interest on pound sterling bank deposits is higher than that currently available on euro bank deposits, why don't European savers change all their money into sterling and put it into British banks?

4

Settling Maturity

GOING BACK TO THE FUTURE

If you have some idea of what you may need to have available at some point in the future, it makes sense to have an appropriate amount of your wealth available at that time. While you can extricate yourself from almost any kind of investment with a little notice, it may turn out to be costly. And why make it more complicated than it needs to be, anyway?

Matching commitments

Look over your commitments list ('Regarding the Future', Chapter 2). See if the list can be ordered by date. It doesn't have to be down to the nearest day! For anything less than a year away, the nearest month will suffice, and for anything further into the future the nearest year will probably suffice.

What this will give you is a pointer to what sort of maturity profile your portfolio could have. As we shall see, it is not the only guide to how you should arrange your investments, but it is a very good place to start. As Figure 5 shows, it can sometimes make the critical difference in choosing between competing investments.

Shading it your way

Future commitments aside, there is no hard-and-fast rule about what the

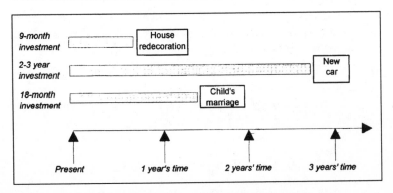

Fig. 5. Matching investments and commitments.

maturity profile of your wealth or investments should look like. Some individuals prefer to have their wealth 'locked up' in financial and non-financial assets that are not about to mature or be sold for quite some time (e.g. five-year investments in National Savings bonds, property). Others like to keep their wealth in assets that have short lives or which can be sold rapidly (e.g. deposit accounts, gold).

Don't disown your natural preferences! Do back them up with reason, however. Where your future commitments give no particular lead, the sections that follow may help you decide what sort of maturity of investment makes sense.

Vanishing profiles

Do remember that the maturity of each investment – and thus the whole portfolio – changes with every passing day! Every investment has a day less to go until it matures, and eventually what was a five-year investment will be a two-year one. If you have set yourself an objective that states that a certain proportion of your wealth should be invested in assets with maturities of more than five years, you will need to top up this class of assets from time to time.

LEAVING ROOM FOR MANOEUVRE

Whatever your future commitments and your natural preferences look like, leave yourself room for manoeuvre! Both of these elements are subject to change, and it would be disappointing to have to sell a profitable investment before you were planning to. You can give yourself room in two ways:

● Keeping part of the portfolio in very short-maturity assets. The most convenient 'investment' in this respect would be an instant-access deposit account of some sort. Even if you don't need such an account for your usual monthly needs, make sure that you can gain access to at least part of your wealth without a performance.

● Choosing investments that mature a little before the money locked up in them is needed. You can always reinvest this money in very short-term assets (as above) from the time the main investments mature until the very day you need it.

COMPLICATING THE ISSUE: YIELD CURVES

One major maturity consideration has nothing to do with your commitments or preferences, and lies completely beyond your control. It consists of a rule that is far from universal but should always be considered. It particularly applies to financial assets: **the longer you tie up your money, the more you can expect to make on it**.

Look at it this way. When you invest your money, you lose the use of it for as long as it remains invested. You do so, of course, because you hope to be paid a return that makes it worth your while. The longer you lose the use of your money, the higher the 'compensation' required. Thus the longer the maturity of your investment – especially if it is a financial one – the higher the reward you should normally expect. Don't rush into long-term financial investments simply because the returns look better than short-term ones! You are gaining more because you are giving up the use of your money for longer, and it isn't *necessarily* worth it.

Understanding yield curves

It is important to realise that where this rule applies, it means rather more than it seems at first sight. The extra return you can expect for having your money tied up for longer is usually higher than what you would get if you put your money in a series of shorter investments, one after the other, to the same ultimate maturity. After all, if you can be assured of the same return for a series of short-term investments (one after the other) as for one long-term one, why would you ever choose the latter?

As we have said, this phenomenon usually applies to financial assets. In the financial world it is often described in terms of **yield curves.** It sounds forbidding, but all a yield curve shows is how much more return you get with increasing maturity, all in graph form. You can draw them yourself, if you find they help you decide what maturity of investment you should go for. In Figure 6 we do just that.

ROLLING FORWARD

There's no reason why your general opinion about the future should be particularly strong. But it could well be that there is something in the future that would make a big difference to what maturities of investments you will prefer. This could be something personal, or something impersonal:

● There could be a future commitment that may not happen at all.

● You may be promoted at an upcoming review at work, giving you extra income.

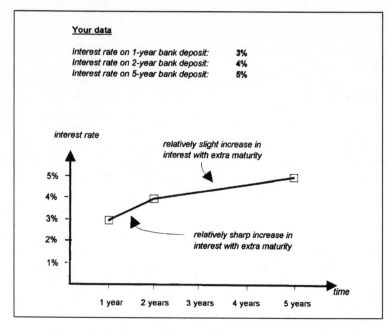

Fig. 6. Drawing a yield curve.

● You may believe that the next general election will make a major difference to economic prospects, one way or the other.

● You may feel that the possible absorption of the pound into the euro will make all the difference to how you invest.

If there is such an unknown (i.e. one with a time limit), there is nothing wrong **with rolling investments forward** until your mind is clearer. This simply means investing them for short maturities and renewing the investment as it expires. A good example would be a **term deposit** (discussed in Chapter 9), which is a bank deposit that has a specified interest rate that will not change for the life of the deposit, but which effectively ties your money up for the agreed period (often one or several months). When this deposit expires you are free to make another one – although possibly at a different rate of interest – if you wish.

STRIKING A BALANCE

Deciding maturities can only be 'scientific' up to a certain point. There are rules such as the general one that the longer you tie your money up, the higher the return you should expect, but in the end the maturity profile of your portfolio is very personal. It may be dictated entirely by your future commitments, or may be very much influenced by your own hunches.

Fortunately, every time you make an investment, you get a chance to alter your overall maturity profile. If you find that your ideas and commitments change, sooner or later you get the chance to make your wealth reflect these changes. In an emergency, you can probably do it more or less at once, but that is something that you would wish to avoid (see Chapter 12). As with risk, if you start off with a balanced portfolio, you will make life easier for yourself.

SUMMARY

1. It makes sense to start thinking about investment maturities with reference to your future commitments as listed in Chapter 2.

2. You may have natural preferences on which maturities you prefer. Don't disown them!

3. The maturity profile of your portfolio will shorten by one day, every day, unless you do something about it.

4. Give yourself room to manoeuvre by keeping some wealth in very short-term assets (e.g. a current account at a bank) and by planning to have investments mature a little before the money invested is required.

5. As a *general* rule, the longer your money is tied up in an investment, the more you should expect to make on it.

6. The extra return you can expect for having your money tied up for longer is usually higher than what you would get if you put your money in a series of shorter investments, one after the other, to the same ultimate maturity.

7. Yield curves show how much more return you get with increasing maturity, all in graph form. You can draw them yourself, for different investments.

8. If you are uncertain about something that may or may not happen on or around a certain future date, consider rolling investments forward until your mind is clearer.

9. The maturity profile of your portfolio is very personal. It may be

dictated entirely by your future commitments, or may be very much influenced by your own hunches.

10. Every time you make a new investment you will be able to alter the maturity profile of your portfolio.

POINTS TO CONSIDER

1. Do you feel that your views on the economy are worth the time of day? Does a journalist necessarily have a better feel for these things than you do?

2. How might a sharp rise in interest paid on deposit accounts affect property prices?

3. In what circumstances might a yield curve for a financial asset be downwards-sloping? In other words, when might the *annual* return on an investment diminish the longer it is held?

5

Grasping the Technical

APPROACHING YOUR CALCULATOR

We have reached the point where a little maths has become indispensable. While risk and maturity can be understood without it, the remaining investment principle – **expected return** – simply cannot. If the concepts presented below are old hat to you, move straight on to Chapter 6. If they are not, something of the technical will do your confidence no harm at all.

Preparing yourself for the job

There are two recommendations when it comes to maths:

1. Open your mind.

2. Equip yourself with a calculator.

The first point is far more important than the second. If you have a facility for maths, the thought of a calculation or two will not bother you. But if you tend to shy away from anything with numbers in it, you must relax and open your mind! Maths isn't magic, just a handy tool lying there and ready for you to use. And as with a washing-machine, a bicycle or a lawnmower, a little practice will make you wonder what the fuss was all about. A calculator isn't a must if you are fond of numbers and are skilled in mental arithmetic. But since investment-related calculations are often repetitive, doing everything longhand may prove rather time-consuming. If you are less than confident about your multiplication tables, however, use a calculator. It doesn't have to be anything fancy! If you have a calculator with a great many functions on it, fine. But any machine that can add, subtract, multiply and divide will be capable of doing the job.

Down to the tenth decimal

Whether you are happy to work everything out longhand or propose to use a calculator, don't get carried away with the accuracy of your calculations. For the purposes of this book, two decimal places will usually suffice. Anything more is wrongheaded. As we shall see, it tends to invest what is possibly only guesswork with unwarranted credibility.

PLAYING WITH PERCENTAGES

Percentages crop up a lot in investment, as they allow easy comparisons to be made. Assume that you are trying to decide between two investments, A and B. They have identical maturities and risks, so only expected return is left for you to make a judgement. Assume further:

● Investment A costs £1,600 and is expected to return £300 in profit.

● Investment B costs £1,900 and is expected to return £350 in profit.

At first glance, it isn't obvious which investment, A or B, is the most profitable. This is where percentages come in.

Stepping through the example

All percentages do is reduce everything to the same scale. In this case, this means the initial cost of the investment and the return. Thus each investment is given a value of 100, and the returns are both expressed as a share of that 100.

● For investment A, the return of 300 is divided by the cost of 1,600. The result, 0.19 (2 decimal places, remember), tells you that the return is worth 0.19 for every 1, you invest. Since we gave the investment a value of 100, we need to multiply both the 1 and the 0.19 by 100 to bring it up to size. Note that by so doing you change nothing of the *relative* size of the return! You now have an investment of 100 (1 × 100) and a return of 19 (0.19 × 100). This 19 is called **19 per cent** (or 19%) because it shows that you will get a return of 19 for every 100 you invest. Every time you see the words 'per cent', this means 'per 100'.

● For investment B, the return of 350 is divided by the cost of 1,900. The result is multiplied by 100, as before, to give a return of **18 per cent**.

Expressing the returns of investment A and investment B as percentages of the initial cost gives you the common basis you need to make an equitable comparison. Your percentage calculation has shown that investment A is slightly more profitable than investment B, despite being smaller in terms of pounds and pence.

Reversing the calculation

If you have a percentage return quoted or an investment, it is a simple matter to obtain from that a return in pounds and pence. You simply work backwards. If an investment is said to have a return of 7 per cent, this means that for every £100 you invest your profit will be £7. If you have £1,500 to invest, this is 15 times 100 (1,500/100 = 15) and therefore the return will be 7 times 15 (to keep everything in the same proportion). Your return on investment is thus £105 (7 × 15 = 105).

In the case of certain financial assets, the procedure can be a little more complex. This is because of what are called **day-counts**. This is something we return to in Chapter 9.

Avoiding the common mistakes

Percentages will work anywhere for comparing returns on investments of different sizes, but there are a couple of pitfalls that you need to avoid:

● Make sure that the return and the cost of the investment are both expressed in the same units to start with. If you are trying to work out what the return on the investment in your house is worth, for example, don't divide £5,000 by '£90k', or 5,000/90! And when it comes to overseas investments, don't muddle up the currencies. Compare like with like.

● If the return on an investment is expressed as a percentage (%) already, don't fiddle with it! By all means convert the percentage back into pounds and pence if you feel like it, but if you're comparing an investment with a return expressed in pounds with another expressed as a percentage, you only need to calculate the percentage return for the first.

COMPOUNDING YOUR INTEREST

There's an illuminating little game that you can play with percentages. Say you have a bank deposit account of £100 today, and assume that the interest you receive on that account is a straightforward 5 per cent a year, credited to your account at the end of each year. If you remain invested in that deposit account for five years, make no withdrawals and interest rates do not change, what will your total return be over that time?

It *isn't* 25 per cent (5 × 5 per cent)! It's more complicated than that, because after the first year you will receive interest on your initial investment *plus* the interest you have already received. In fact, your annual returns will be as follows:

● Year 1: deposit of £100, 5 per cent interest returns £5 (5/100 × 100)

● Year 2: deposit of £105 (100 + 5), 5 per cent interest returns £5.25.

- Year 3: deposit of £110.25, 5 per cent interest returns £5.51 (5/100 × 110.25, rounded to 2 decimal places).

- Year 4: deposit of £115.76, 5 per cent interest returns £5.79.

- Year 5: deposit of £121.55, 5 per cent interest returns £6.08. After five years, therefore, the account has a balance of £127.63 (121.55 + 6.08).

Of this balance of £127.63, your original investment was £100. The return on investment is thus £27.63 (127.63 − 100), or **27.63 per cent**. Not 25 per cent!

The thing is, whenever you are paid a periodic return on your investment and you add that return to your original investment (**you reinvest the proceeds**, in the jargon), you will *always* generate a higher return than if you withdraw it. This phenomenon is known as **compound interest**. (Some calculators will generate compound interest for you, without you having to determine interest for each year, one after the other. But don't rush out to get one, if yours doesn't do it. It's not that hard!)

A secondary point is that the return on five years – almost 28 per cent – looks very dramatic. So it is, and all from a modest annual interest rate! The next time someone tells you about a fantastic five-year investment that will give you your money back plus 25 per cent (or something even more impressive), it's not necessarily that hot! You may be able to get that sort of a return down at your local bank.

STANDARDISING RETURNS

Turning all expected returns into percentages is only part of what you have to do to make valid comparisons. The way in which the returns are calculated on investments might be different: how can you be sure that an investment returning 20 per cent in three years' time is a better deal than one returning 6 per cent per year for three years?

Selecting your standard

You will often see returns on investments – and especially financial ones – expressed as so many per cent per year. But there is no *mathematical* reason why you should have to compare returns on an annual basis too. Indeed, unless you are mathematically minded, you might find it fiddly to do so.

If you have selected the maturity of investment you want *before* you consider returns, you might as well compare all the alternatives before you on the basis of that maturity. The important point is not so much what the maturity is, but that you compare the alternative investments on the *same basis* (i.e. to the same maturity).

Tackling the question
The first investment mentioned above (the one returning 20 per cent in three years' time) demands no calculations. If you are looking for a three-year investment, the return on this one is already expressed on that basis. The second one is expressed annually, and therefore needs adjustment. What does a 6 per cent annual return mean over three years?

The calculation is one of compounding, as in the previous section:

- Give the initial cost of the investment a value of 100, irrespective of what it actually is.

- Compound the interest over three years, as in the previous section (thus year 1, deposit of 100, interest of $6/100 \times 100 = 6$; year 2, deposit of 106, interest of $6/100 \times 106$, etc.).

- The total of investment plus interest at the end of year 3 should be 119.10. Since you started with only 100, the difference (19.10) is the return on the investment. '19.10 per 100' is the same thing as '19.1 per cent'.

The second investment returns just over 19 per cent over three years, slightly less than the 20 per cent for the first investment. The first is therefore the most profitable.

Decompounding returns (optional – only for the bold)
It was mentioned that expressing diverse returns on annual bases could be fiddly. If you aren't frightened of the fiddly, you might have already wondered why you couldn't **decompound** (as well as compound) interest. For it may be that you would prefer to standardise everything to annual returns, irrespective of the actual maturity of the investment.

Go back to the question of an investment returning 20 per cent in three years' time against one returning 6 per cent per year for three years. Since we have chosen one year as the standard basis of comparison, the second asset needs no conversion. It is the first that requires decompounding. In other words, we need to discover what the annual return would be that would generate 20 per cent over three years. Note that nobody is saying that the return on this asset has to be regular. It may earn little for the first two years and then a lot all in the last year. All we are doing is assuming that the return *is* regular in order to make a comparison with another asset.

In brief, there are three ways of arriving at the answer. The way you choose depends largely on the complexity of your calculator:

1. The easiest – use a decompounding function on a 'scientific' calculator. If you don't know how to use the function, look it up in the manual.

2. Decompound using the '×√' function. Express the three-year return in the example as 0.20, add the initial cost (1), and perform the following calculation: 3√1.20, which gives you 1.0627 (to 4 decimal places). Remove the 1 again (the initial investment cost) and express what is left as a percentage (i.e. multiply by 100). The result is 6.27 per cent.

3. If you have neither of the above functions on your calculator, you can get the answer by an iterative process. This can be rather time-consuming, of course. You *guess* what the annual return might be that gives you 20 per cent after three years, compound the interest on the basis of that guess, and adjust that guess in the light of how far above or below 20 per cent you turn out to be. The calculation is repeated until you are close enough for your own satisfaction.

BUYING AND SELLING

The technicalities of investment are not purely mathematical. This is the case for buying and selling, activities that appear straightforward enough but cause a surprising amount of confusion.

Companies that earn money by buying and selling assets – especially financial assets – will often have two prices for the same asset. They will **buy** an asset for one price and **sell** it for another, higher, price. Since they often quote both prices, not knowing in advance whether any given customer is about to buy or sell, you may not know which is which. If you calculate what an investment is going to cost, using the wrong price (i.e. the price at which you can sell, not where you can buy), your calculation will be inaccurate. And you could mess up any expected return calculation as well.

Three key terms

Some jargon is unavoidable here. Most institutions that deal with the public are much more consumer-friendly than they used to be. They make it clear which price is their buying price and which is their selling price (the same applies to the *Financial Times*, incidentally). In case they don't, remember the following:

● The **bid** (or bid price) **is where the dealer** (bank, stockbroker, etc.) **will buy** the asset concerned. If they are *buying*, you must be *selling*. You cannot buy the asset from that dealer at that price.

● The **offer** (or offer price, occasionally 'ask') **is where the dealer will sell** the asset. If they are *selling*, you must be *buying*. You cannot sell the asset to that dealer at that price.

There is an easy way to recall which price applies to you. It is always the worst of the two prices! If you are buying, it is always the higher of the two prices, and if you are selling, it is the lower.

The difference between the buying and selling price for the same asset is known as the **spread**. The next time you walk into a High Street bank, look for a board with the bank's exchange rates on it. If there is such a board, you will see that the bank quotes different exchange rates depending on whether they are buying pounds off you (and selling a foreign currency to you) or selling pounds to you (and buying a foreign currency off you). This difference is their spread on foreign currency transactions.

HANDLING DIFFERENT CURRENCIES

There's plenty of scope for getting muddled up with foreign currencies. As you may have already found out, mistakes never seem to work to your advantage! Fortunately, one very simple idea will help you avoid most of them.

The **base currency** is the currency that is worth 1 against an amount of a foreign currency. If you walk into a British bank, you may find that the bank is prepared to buy pounds for 1.60 US dollars. This means that you will get 1.60 dollars for every pound you sell to the bank (ignoring commissions). If you kept your pounds in your pocket and went to the United States with them, and walked into an American bank, you might find that they will buy your pounds (and sell you dollars) at '0.625'. Have exchange rates gone crazy here?

They haven't gone crazy. All that has happened is that the base currency has changed. In Britain, logically enough, foreign currencies are quoted per £1 . The pound is the base currency. In the United States, the dollar is the base currency and foreign currencies (including the pound, of course) are quoted per $1. 1.60 dollars per pound is *exactly the same* as 0.625 pounds per dollar.

(It may interest you to know that international currency markets have standard base currencies. This avoids confusion where dealers are speaking from different countries and have different 'natural' base currencies.)

Dealing with euros

Since 1 January 1999, eleven European countries have fixed their national currencies against a new one – the euro. As you may know, non-cash transactions within these countries may be carried out in euros, and in 2002 the eleven national currencies will vanish altogether. It may be that Britain, too, will adopt the new currency one day.

Replacing lots of currencies with just one makes life simpler if you plan to invest in Europe. Don't complicate it all over again! If you want to make one investment in Germany and another in France, for example, you only need to change your pounds once (assuming you're not using cash)! A euro is a euro: there's no such thing as a French euro and a German one.

FACTORING IN TAXES

Any calculation you make about investments should take taxes into account. Since some investments are not taxable, and others are, you will not be comparing like with like if you leave taxes out of it.

When you come to calculate expected returns, adjust them by any tax you expect to pay. The easiest way to do this is to work out the amount of tax you will pay in pounds and pence, either during each year of the asset's life or, if appropriate, at maturity. You then subtract it from the expected return (again, in pounds and pence) before going on to any percentage calculations.

If you are comparing two assets that are taxed in exactly the same way (two bank deposits, for example), you need not perform the above calculation. They are comparable as they are.

SUMMARY

1. To get the most out of the maths, open your mind and equip yourself with a calculator. The first is indispensable, the second doesn't apply to people who really love working everything out longhand.

2. Two decimal places is usually more than enough accuracy for the purposes of this book.

3. All percentages do is reduce everything to the same scale. This allows comparisons to be made.

4. 19 per cent means 19 per 100, or 19/100. It may be expressed as 19%.

5. If you reinvest the interest you receive on an asset, you will compound this interest. Compounding at even modest interest rates can generate surprisingly high returns after a few years.

6. Compare the returns on different investments by making sure they all refer to the same maturity.

7. Where two prices for the same asset are quoted, one will be the dealer's bid and the other the dealer's offer. The bid is where the dealer will buy from you. and the offer is where they will sell to you. Make sure you make your calculations using the correct price.

8. The gap between a dealer's bid and offer prices is the dealer's spread.

9. The base currency in a foreign exchange transaction is usually the currency of the country you are in. All other currencies are quoted per 1 unit (pound, dollar, euro, etc) of the base currency.

10. Some investments are not taxable. while others are. You will not be comparing like with like if you leave taxes out of your calculations.

POINTS TO CONSIDER

1. Assume that you have a credit card that charges 2 per cent interest per month on unpaid accounts, and that you leave £100 unpaid. How long will it take for that debt of £100 to double if interest rates do not change?

2. What does a wide bid–offer spread tell you about the competitiveness of the dealer?

3. Why do you always seem to lose money when you change unused foreign holiday money back into pounds?

6

Exploring Expected Return

UNDERSTANDING THE CONCEPT

In Chapter 3 we outlined the three investment principles that will be your guide in managing your own money. You will recall that you can look at an investment – or your portfolio as a whole – in terms of maturity, expected return and risk. You may also have gathered that you are going to deal with your own investments by applying all three principles to any new investment.

Of the three principles, expected return has been saved until last. It needed a touch of the maths, for one thing. It is perhaps a little more controversial than the others, too.

Worrying about objectivity

We need to use **expected return** rather than simply **return** because the latter can only refer to the past or present, and investment is concerned with the future. Of course, how an investment has performed in the past is often a good pointer to how it will behave in the future, but, as any horse-racing fan will tell you, there's usually a lot more to it.

In principle, expected return works in the same way as you might expect 'actual' return to work. It operates with the other two investment principles in the following way:

● you take a number of investments of the same maturity

● you discard those investments that appear too risky for you

● you express the expected returns of the investments that remain as percentages

● you choose the investment with the highest expected return.

You may have nagging worries about the apparent simplicity of this approach. You might concede that expected return is the best we can do to compare the future profitability of two investments, but the lack of objectivity may worry you. You can see that maturity is objective. You may feel that risk depends to some extent on the 'eye of the beholder', but in general you can expect most people to agree on which of two investments is the riskier. But expected return? If I say that house prices in your area will rise by 20 per cent in one year, who are you to say they won't?

Expecting and predicting

You won't get rid of subjectivity in investment, no matter how hard you try. If investment were simply a matter of comparing facts, no judgement would ever be required and everyone who felt like it would be wealthy!

Expected return is where most of your own thinking fits in. If you don't feel comfortable with your own thoughts, one wonders why you thought you could manage your own money. At some point your opinion has to be brought to bear. And that point has arrived...

If 'expected' is too strong, try 'predicted'. If you're not confident enough to say that you *expect* so-and-so to happen, you will be able to live with *predicting* it. As far as investment is concerned, one is as good as the other.

IDENTIFYING RETURN ON INVESTMENT

Estimating the return on an investment may involve two distinct elements:

1. The income you may receive on it. As you can see from Figure 7, this includes interest, dividends and, in the case of property, rent.

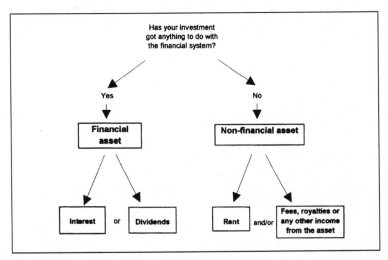

Fig. 7. Types of investment income.

2. The increase or decrease in underlying value (i.e. the difference between initial cost and final value) between the time you invest and the maturity date.

Handling any income

Not all investments generate income before they mature. If an investment does generate an income, it should be included in final return. And if it is *reinvested*, it should be compounded as shown in Chapter 5.

Separating underlying value

The underlying value of an investment is its cost, as determined by a market or as judged in your mark-to-market (Chapter 2). As with investment income, underlying value may or may not be relevant to assessing expected return. There are three possible cases:

1. No change in underlying value. The investment is worthwhile because of the income it generates before it matures. For example, if you invest £1,000 in a bank deposit, the underlying value of that investment will always be £1,000 (assuming the bank stays solvent). The return on that investment is all accounted for by the interest income it generates.

2. The underlying value changes, and there is no investment income at all. If you buy gold coins, for example, you will receive no income from them. Your final return depends entirely on the underlying value of the asset (the price of gold, and possibly any scarcity value of the coins you have bought).

3. The underlying value changes *and* there is investment income. This is true of purchases of shares, for example. You receive dividends as a shareholder, and the underlying value of the shares (the share price multiplied by the number of shares you own) may move from day to day.

Be clear about what sort of returns your investment is generating. Some returns may be stated in advance, some require you to come up with a prediction. Is the return on the investment under consideration purely investment income, purely changes in underlying value, or some combination of the two? Asking yourself this question every time you invest will ensure that you do not leave any part of its final return out of the equation.

REINVESTING RETURNS

Be very careful about what you do with investment income. There is no reason why you can't treat it like any other income (see Chapter 1) and have it available to spend. That's up to you. But you can't have your cake and eat it!

If your final return calculation assumes that you are reinvesting your investment income, *reinvest it*. It may be that the profitability of the investment depends on it.

Placing income on deposit

If you're thinking that reinvesting income from an investment only applies to the interest you receive on a bank deposit, think again. If you have rental income, or dividends from shares you own, for example, why should these sums not be placed in your deposit account and compounded as if they were interest income?

PUTTING NUMBERS ON HUNCHES

It follows from the above that coming up with an 'expectation' for expected return may involve estimating two different things: **investment income** and **underlying value**. It is possible that the two things are linked, but usually they are not, and keeping the two concepts separate will avoid needless muddle.

Guessing investment income

Investment income need not be very complicated to estimate. It may be something you can determine (rent on property you own), something specified in advance (the interest on a fixed-term bank deposit), or something that may not have changed too much in the past and is unlikely to change dramatically in the future (dividend payments on some shares). And, as we have seen, some investments generate no income at all.

The investment that will give you most pause for thought will be floating-rate bank deposits. These are any bank deposits where the interest rate is not agreed in advance, which is the case for most bank accounts. Income from these accounts varies with interest rates generally. If you are considering investing some of your money in a standard deposit account, therefore, you need to come up with an idea of where interest rates are heading. **And if you have no idea, why are you so keen on this investment?**

Matching underlying value with maturity

Whenever you invest money, you need to know both how much you propose to spend (the initial cost of the investment) and how much you expect to be returned to you at maturity (the final value). As we have seen, some assets have maturities already built in (a National Savings bond, for example), while others do not come with maturities ready-made and it is up to you to assign them (shares, for example). It bears repeating that you should *always* have a final maturity date in mind for an investment. Holding onto an asset 'until it makes money' is very poor management since it is almost always inefficient.

The final value at maturity is what *you* expect to be returned at the end of the investment period. This may not necessarily involve guesswork, since the return on some assets is fixed in advance (again, as with National Savings bonds). But for the most part it is up to you to sit down and figure out what you think will happen. If you don't know where to start, use the following as a guide:

● Remember what we talked about in Chapter 4 in connection with deciding the maturity of investment you wanted. You can use it here too. Do you feel that people like you – buyers of assets, that is – are going to get better-off or worse-off during the life of the investment?

● If the asset you are looking at has performed well in the past, do you think that the conditions in which it thrived will be repeated in the future?

● Are there any political or social developments that will have a bearing on the asset under consideration? Does it depend on fashion, and might that change?

Whatever your reasoning, come up with a final value. This gives you an estimate of any change in the underlying value of the investment.

A BASIS FOR COMPARISON

We conclude this chapter with a few worked examples of calculating expected return. Assume that you are considering investing £500 for three years (**maturity** is defined), and there are three assets that you like the look of and which are not too risky for you (**risk** is acceptable). The investment decision will therefore be entirely dependent on a comparison of expected returns.

Assume further that the three assets are as follows:

- 500 shares in XYZ plc, on offer at 100p each

- a deposit account in your local High Street bank

- a case of vintage Bordeaux, stored in a climate-controlled warehouse in France.

We evaluate the expected return on each asset in turn.

Asset 1: XYZ shares

Note that we have started off on the right foot by using the **offer** price of the shares, not the bid price. We have stated that the investment is to have a three-year maturity, which means that you plan to sell these shares in three years' time.

The question, as always, is the following: *Is the return on the investment purely investment income, purely changes in underlying value or some combination of the two?* In this case the answer is 'some combination of the two', since shares both generate income (dividends) and are subject to changes in their underlying value (i.e. price).

- You need to estimate the dividends you can expect to receive from XYZ Company. Dividends are explored in some detail in Chapter 9, so don't worry at this stage if you aren't sure what they are or how you might go about estimating what they might be in the future. Suffice to say that you need to make sure that your dividend return takes account of any tax you may have to pay on them, and don't forget to consider whether these dividends are to be reinvested. If they are, compound them as shown in Chapter 6. *Assume that you come up with an estimate of investment income that is worth 10 per cent of your investment after three years.*

- You need to estimate the share price of XYZ Company in three years' time. How do you think this share will behave? How has it behaved in the past? Do you think that the conditions that gave the company that past performance will be better or worse in the future? What do the experts or financial press think? Remember, if you don't have any view on what might happen to this share price, you shouldn't be investing in this company! *Assume that you conclude that the share price will be 120p in three years' time. The change in the underlying value is 20 (120 – 100), and therefore the return is 20/100, or 20 per cent.*

- Expected return for the share investment is therefore 30 per cent after three years (10 + 20).

Asset 2: a deposit account

As with asset 1, you need to ask whether investment income and changes in underlying value are relevant here.

- The investment income on a deposit account is the interest you will receive. As we saw in Chapter 5, it makes a big difference to your return whether you reinvest the interest payments or not. As far as estimating a return is concerned, you will have to consider what interest rates are likely to be in the three years ahead. Whether you have a firm grasp of economics or simply go with what you feel, your opinion is paramount. Don't assume that estimating future interest rates is a piece of cake, by the way. The world's financial markets are trying to do that all the time, and with limited success! And remember to allow for any tax you may have to pay on your interest. *Assume that you conclude that you will be paid interest (after the bank has deducted the tax payable) at an annual rate of 4 per cent in year 1, 5 per cent in year 2 and 6 per cent in year 3. Compound this interest, and your return in three years will be 15.75 per cent. Check this figure!*

- The underlying value of a bank deposit does not usually change. The **principal,** as it is called, will be £500 from start to finish of your three-year investment period. So long as your bank stays solvent (remember your risk rules!), only commissions or fees would affect your principal. If there are any commissions levied by the bank (unlikely), make sure you know what they are. *Assume that you conclude that your underlying value will not change. This element of expected return will therefore be zero.*

- Expected return for the bank deposit is therefore 15.75 per cent after three years (15.75 + 0).

Asset 3: a case of fine wine

As we stressed at the beginning of this book, there is no reason why non-financial investments cannot be evaluated in the same way as financial ones. Your wealth is not all financial, and there is no good reason why it should be. Many wine connoisseurs follow the market for fine wines closely enough to have a nose for a good opportunity when they see one, and will buy not just for their own consumption (current spending, as defined in Chapter 1) but for investment purposes too.

As before, the question is as follows: *Is the return on the investment purely investment income, purely changes in underlying value, or some combination of the two?*

- There is unlikely to be any investment income on a case of wine. *This element of expected return will therefore be zero.*

- The underlying value of the wine will almost certainly change. As with the shares, you need to use your own judgement, experience and research to come up with a figure for the value for the case in three years' time. You will need to subtract from that figure any storage charges and tax you will have to pay. *Assume that you conclude that the price of your case of wine will be £750 in three years' time, and that you will have to pay £50 in storage charges and taxes. The change in the underlying value is 200   (750 – 50 – 500), and therefore the return is 200/500, or 40 per cent.*

- Expected return for the case of wine is therefore 40 per cent after three years (0 + 40).

Loading up with wine

Your comparison of three assets on the basis of expected return (they were all suitable under maturity and risk considerations, remember) produced a clear result. The case of wine is the most profitable investment (40 per cent return after three years), followed by shares in XYZ Company (30 per cent return) and then a bank deposit (15.75 per cent return).

Nobody wants to spoil the party. But before you rush into wine, pause for one moment. If this investment is so much more profitable than the alternatives you considered, why isn't *everyone* buying wine?

It may well be that you've spotted a great opportunity. Good luck to you! No harm in double-checking your assumptions, though...

SUMMARY

1. Expected return is the third of the three investment principles that may be used to evaluate different investments. The other two, of course, are maturity and risk.

2. We use **expected return** rather than simply **return** because the latter can only refer to the past or present, and investment is concerned with the future.

3. Expected return is often subjective. It doesn't make it less valid than maturity or risk for choosing between investments, however. Your own judgement has to come in somewhere.

4. The expected return on an investment to a given maturity date may have two elements: **investment income,** and **change in underlying value**. Some investments have one of these elements, and some have both.

5. If an investment does generate an income, it may or may not be reinvested. If you are relying on reinvestment to give you your final return, then reinvest!

6. If you have rental income or dividends from shares, you can place these sums in a deposit account and compound them just as if they were interest income.

7. The underlying value of an investment is its cost, as determined by a market or as judged in your mark-to-market.

8. If you have no idea what either investment income or change in underlying value is for a given investment, you shouldn't be considering it.

9. Remember to include taxes and any charges or commissions in your expected return calculations.

10. The expected return on assets as diverse as shares and a case of wine may be evaluated in the same way and therefore compared directly.

POINTS TO CONSIDER

1. Can asset prices ever change if the experts know what is going to happen?

2. Why might a rational investor plump for a bank deposit expecting to return 15 per cent over three years and walk away from the case of wine that is expected to return 40 per cent? What elementary risk rule would *always* make him or her do that? (*Hint: it's listed in Chapter 2.*) Does this rule appeal to you?

3. What is the expected return on doing nothing with your money? Is doing nothing an investment decision?

7

Competing with Experts

APPRECIATING EXPERTISE

Investment experts of whatever type are not called experts for nothing. Many of them, after all, are required by law to pass nationally recognised examinations before they are allowed to advise you. But they are not experts in *everything*, and to be fair, they rarely claim to be. Take a look at the various fields in which investment advisers might specialise:

- pensions

- unit trusts

- the stock market

- the property market

- overseas investments

- precious metals

- collectibles, such as antiques.

The list is hardly exhaustive. What it shows, however, is that you should 'pick horses for courses'. The trick is to lean on experts for the things they know, and for nothing else.

Sticking to safe ground

Let's take an example. Somebody competent to advise you on the stock market can be of tremendous help in a number of ways. But these ways are **specific**, and once you stray into other things the expert's opinion is not necessarily more valuable than anybody else's.

- **This expert can explain:**
    - financial statistics
    - investment regulations
    - current market prices
    - relevant history
    - the performance of similar shares.

● **This expert cannot tell you:**
  - whether you should buy or not
  - what a particular company will decide
  - what market prices will be
  - what future company profits will be
  - whether you should buy a painting instead.

If you keep the experts corralled within their areas of expertise, you will gain by their advice. Questions of the future, as we shall see, are *not* within their competence, and neither are investments which they do not follow. **Don't muddle facts with speculation.** In any case, as remarked upon in Chapters 3 and 5, speculation with your money is *your* job, not somebody else's.

Selecting the good bits

Sadly, a great many investment advisers of all types like to talk more than they like to listen. There may be good reasons for this (see below), but it's not always easy to confine them to facts that you want to know. Often politeness prevents us from interrupting, and we end up too swamped or muddled to move.

A good way to cope with this situation is to **take notes**. This applies whether you are on the telephone or face-to-face with an adviser. Follow the steps listed below:

1. Write down – in abbreviated form – the various points that are made to you. If they are too long, or don't make sense, don't write them down at all.

2. When the conversation is over, sit down with your notes and mark each point with the comment 'Fact' or 'Opinion'.

3. Consider the 'Facts' and ask yourself whether any are **outside the adviser's area of expertise**. If they are, they should either be crossed out or checked with another source.

4. Consider the 'Opinions'. Cross out any that do not seem **to you** to be interesting or worth further thought.

5. On a clean sheet, write out the 'Facts' and 'Opinions' that remain.

This approach has several advantages:

● It forces you to be rigorous about what is factual and what is not.

● If you are face-to-face, the act of taking notes may in itself keep your adviser to the point.

● You waste no time on points that make no sense or are too complicated to be of use.

● You are forced to take your time about committing to anything (see below).

None of the above is supposed to dissuade you from asking for advice! But it is vital that you discern fact from opinion, and sense from a verbal haemorrhage. Habits such as the taking and then pruning of notes not only get you closer to the answers to your questions. They sharpen you up in general.

DIGGING FOR ASSUMPTIONS

Economic or financial commentators on the television and radio are an impressive group of people. They are knowledgeable, articulate, and appear to have their fingers on the pulse of the world's markets. Newscasters fire questions at them about Japanese unemployment or gold prices, and polished, convincing answers come back with scarcely a moment's hesitation. People whom you talk to about your investments may be like that too. How dare you doubt what they tell you?

Inspecting the foundations
You *can* dare, because the most sophisticated arguments often depend on simple facts or opinions. The language of investment and economics in general has a great many obscure terms and can sound most daunting. But at the root of it all are simple assertions that anyone can readily understand.

It's a little bit like looking at a great cathedral. The complexity and elegance of the structure soaring over your head may impress you. It may seem to you that you could never understand how it is done. But if you look *down* for a moment, at the great stones that support the columns, the buttresses or the walls, you can see at once that the whole thing depends on something very basic. And that all the elegance over your head will collapse if you take out just one of those very simple square blocks at your feet.

It's all a question of **digging**. If someone tells you that such-and-such an investment is wise, ask why. If you don't understand the reason, say so. There is nothing foolish in asking such questions:

● It is amazing how quickly you can get to the root of the whole matter, down to the simplest assertions that you can agree or disagree with.

- It can tell you whether your adviser has actually thought the whole thing through, rather than simply repeating something he or she heard.

Asking the right questions

There is no need for you to study economics at night or to try and pretend that you know more than you do. When you are given investment advice, the best questions are honest ones. They are also the most unnerving for experts to answer, funnily enough.

Take another example. If someone advises you to invest in commercial property (via a unit trust, say – see Chapter 9), because some cycle is 'at a low' and because 'occupancy rates are climbing', you can get to the heart of the matter without having any specialist knowledge yourself. Your questions might include the following:

- What is an occupancy rate?

- What is this cycle? How long has it been observed, and has each 'low' been as obvious as this one?

- What drives this cycle?

- How do you know that occupancy rates are not about to *stop* climbing?

- Does a greater use of information technology (allowing people to work from home) mean that less rather than more office space is required?

These need not be your preferred questions, and you might think of additional ones. The point remains that questions that sound naive and non-technical are often the best ones for getting to the centre of the issue.

Leaning on experience

Getting down to the basic building blocks of what an expert is telling you has a point. It is not simply to understand it all better, important though that is. **It is the means by which you place advice face-to-face with your own experience.**

TRUSTING YOUR JUDGEMENT

Your willingness to throw questions at experts depends in the end on how far you trust your own judgement in the management of your own money. If you are serious about taking charge, you will inevitably want to get to the bottom of what you are being told. If you ask no questions, and allow yourself to be dazzled by jargon, you are no longer in control.

Think of yourself as a judge, presiding over a complex case in which there is no jury. It is all up to you. There are expert witnesses, as many as you need. If you ask them questions, if you get them to explain what they mean, does this make you look foolish? Of course not. On the contrary – it makes you look **wise**. And if you simply nod at what they tell you, why not be done with it and leave the judging to them too?

Taking pride in yourself

It's all very well in theory, you may say, but actually putting questions to experts and asking them to justify and explain is still daunting. They know so much…

It is, of course, a matter of confidence. Remind yourself of the things you know and which the expert probably does not. You may not see yourself as an expert in *anything*, but it's almost impossible to grow up and walk around as an adult without becoming an expert in *something*. It could be related to your job, to your hobbies, to any sports you follow or practise, to raising your children. And the next time people advise you on what they know, don't hesitate to ask those questions. You know things they never will.

PREDICTING THE FUTURE

The belief that we humans can know what the future holds is an ancient one. It is a belief that has defied reason for centuries, and clings to us even today. Some of us are open about it, consulting fortune-tellers and the like; others scoff at the idea yet turn to the newspaper horoscopes first thing in the morning. And if a prophecy is clothed in scientific language, so much the better. Millions will swallow it without a second thought.

It is amazing just how many people seem to know what will happen to your money if you put it into this or that. And how helpful they can be in getting it there! Call them experts if you like. But whether you believe in divination or not, keep your hand on your wallet. At least until you have finished this section…

Believing in magic

If you *must* believe in magic, keep your money out of it. It is one thing to be wary of a tall dark stranger and quite another to give him all you own. If anyone proposes an investment to you that depends for its return on a particular turn of future events, don't accept that particular turn as fact. **It can't be.**

Beware, too, of investment strategies that sound like good ideas but which depend on magic all the same:

- anything based on tax changes that the Chancellor 'will announce' in the next Budget

- anything that urges you to buy now, 'before the Japanese do'

- anything that claims to profit from an 'imminent' financial crisis.

None of these sorts of strategies need be unwise. The point is that the future event in each case is an unknown, and you ought to apply that to the risk criteria you have already set yourself (Chapter 2). By all means gamble if you wish, but be aware that it *is* a gamble, and not a guaranteed outcome. No magic. Okay?

Trusting the priesthood

In the late Roman Republic, priests were often up-and-coming politicians who used their office as a stepping-stone to greater things. They jostled for these prestigious and useful positions with a ruthlessness that would do credit to a modern day MP. The thing is, the moment they were installed in office they were credited with all sorts of prophetic powers, powers that they would never have claimed before their appointment.

Investment advisers can be like that. They get up in the morning and look like ordinary men and women, no more likely to tell the future than you or I. But they put on their business suits, and lo and behold! We can't agree with their predictions fast enough. Like the Roman, we really ought to get behind their trappings. Would we be so quick to trust what they predict if they were dressed in a scruffy pair of weekend jeans? If not, why not? Is it not because they would look just like us, with exactly the same prophetic powers as we have?

Ignoring the past

History is absolutely *packed* with the howlers of prophets, financial and otherwise. Indeed, it is probable that every disaster or financial collapse there has ever been was preceded by some expert saying that things were looking better than ever!

Sadly, even the most well-informed do not have privileged access to the future. Next time you read the financial press, stick to what it tells you about what is happening **now** or what has happened **before**. The rest is no more worthwhile than what that gypsy at the fairground has to say.

LISTENING, NOT COMMITTING

Being prepared to listen to an expert is a perfectly sound way of obtaining information, especially if you are prepared to question what they are saying. But do not fall into the trap of committing yourself as soon as the expert has finished talking. *Always* give yourself time to think it over. If the expert is recommending a rapid decision, all the more reason to slow down! The chances of you really missing something are *extremely* remote.

Arranging appointments

Slowing everything down has two outstanding advantages:

1. It gives you time to apply the three investment principles (maturity, expected return and risk) to whatever is proposed. **Does the 'deal' make sense for you?**

2. It gives you a chance to formulate questions, i.e. **do some digging**.

An excellent way of slowing everything down is simply to arrange an appointment to discuss things further. This would work just as well with an adviser speaking to you on the phone as it would if you were face to face. Simply explain that you wish to think things over and will make a decision at your leisure. If this appears unacceptable to the adviser, you have probably learned something worth knowing straight off...

Falling for favouritism

You might recall one of the 'points to consider' at the end of Chapter 3: why would an investment adviser show *you* the bargain of the century? If someone calls you to say that there is a great opportunity that is being shown to you first – and you had better snap it up fast – ask yourself why the caller is doing you such a favour. More to the point, why don't those with great bargains on offer snap them up themselves?

Sadly, whenever money is involved people tend not to do you favours.

Ringing around

There is nothing illegal about double-checking a piece of investment advice! If you have taken time to think the matter over, applied your three investment principles to what is being proposed, and find that it suits but you still have nagging doubts, ask some other expert. You need not say who you got the original piece of advice from. But another opinion won't hurt. There is more than one specialist in every field, from shares to fine art. Most are delighted to give you advice, since you may turn to them next time.

SUMMARY

1. No expert is an expert in everything. Pick horses for courses.

2. Experts can help you in many ways. But these ways are specific, even on their own subject.

3. Take notes of investment advice. If the point is too long or complicated, don't bother with it, and separate fact from opinion.

4. No matter how high-flown and technical an argument sounds, it always rests on simple facts or assumptions. Dig them out.

5. Don't be afraid of asking basic questions. These are often the most pertinent and are also the most effective at finding weak spots.

6. Trust your own judgement. Think of yourself as a presiding judge in court: the expert witnesses are there to help you, but at the end of the day it is not they who pass sentence.

7. If you must believe in prophecies and other magic, keep your money out of it. The future is in the lap of the gods, not at the beck and call of investment experts.

8. History is packed with howlers as far as predicting the future is concerned. And they can't be all finished.

9. Don't rush to commit yourself to an investment. Always give yourself time to think it over – on your own!

10. Investment professionals are not in the business of doing favours. Be wary of anyone who claims to be doing you one.

POINTS TO CONSIDER

1. If your personal life were being probed, whose questions would you most fear: an adult's or a child's? Do children ask more stupid questions than adults do?

2. Whenever you sat written examinations at school or elsewhere, did any of the stronger candidates cover their desks with lucky charms?

3. Do you look down on people who ask you for advice? If they question your advice, does that make them smaller still?

8

Getting It Together

STARTING FROM SOMEWHERE

Managing your own money, as you have seen, involves no little attention to detail. The chapters up until now have been concerned with that detail, especially as it relates to the three investment principles you will use. Inevitably, however, the explanation of the bits and pieces will have made it difficult to see how everything fits together. This is what we are about to do now.

Measuring the flows
Right at the start you were encouraged to think of your wealth as the contents of a fish tank, with water coming in (income) and water flowing out (spending). You noted the various financial and non-financial assets that made up your wealth, and were told to keep track of your income and spending flows because the balance between them would affect your wealth. Furthermore, you were advised to make a distinction between current spending and investment, the former being spending that you 'consumed' and the latter being merely the exchange of one form of wealth for another.

The point of all this was to give you an idea of where you were starting from. You can't manage your wealth at all unless you know *both* of the following:

● how much you have

● whether what you have is increasing or decreasing with your monthly income and spending.

Recording your numbers
You may remember that your record-keeping was not simply about tracking income and spending every month. It also included marking-to-market, which is a regular update on the value of those assets you count as your wealth.

You may have realised that the mark-to-market exercise is not only about keeping tabs on what you have, vital though that is. It also serves to track the performance of your investments, a point we shall return to in Chapter 11.

STICKING TO YOUR GUIDELINES

From very early on there was mention of **writing things down**. There are five sorts of things that you ought to record. Including the items just mentioned, these are as follows:

1. your list of assets available for management and the associated monthly mark-to-market

2. your tracking of income and spending

3. your future financial commitments, where known

4. your personal objectives in managing your own money

5. where these are not included in the above, your risk limits.

The first two items keep you informed of where you are, and the last three are your guidelines as you go forward. You were invited to refer to these guidelines whenever you were listening to advice or researching possible investments, since they could stop you straying off into places you shouldn't be.

Your guidelines serve as a sort of screen. What they will do is stop you wasting your time with investments that are not going to be suitable for you. Thus only those investments that qualify under your guidelines get as far as being assessed by the three investment principles.

WEIGHTING YOUR ASSETS

Your financial and non-financial wealth items may all be referred to as your **assets** or your **portfolio**. These assets, as well as any new ones you are thinking of buying, may be assessed using three investment principles: maturity, expected return and risk.

Recall what each investment principle is about:

● **Maturity** is the term of the investment. It is the length of time between now and the moment the investment expires or is to be sold. Remember that whatever the maturity of the investment at the date of purchase, it falls a little with each passing day.

● **Expected return** is your opinion of what the return of the investment will be to maturity. This has two elements: investment income and change in underlying value. Some investments may have only one of these elements. Expected return is expressed as a percentage for the sake of easy comparison.

● **Risk** is your assessment of how safe your money will be when it is tied up in any particular investment. Although nothing on the planet is 100 per cent certain, some investments are plainly riskier than others. And some are not risky in themselves, but are open to **translation risk** (investments in foreign currencies).

You use the three principles in turn to weigh the suitability of a particular investment or to look at the shape of your wealth as a whole (your portfolio). Each principle involves your opinions or preferences to a lesser or greater extent:

● Your maturity preferences will depend on your future commitments, your desire to keep some room for manoeuvre, your general optimism or pessimism about the economy in general, and the general rule that the longer your money is tied up, the more you should expect to earn on it.

● The 'expected' in expected return is what *you* expect. You may well take advice, but in the end it is something you are going to decide. If you cannot come up with any idea of an expected return for a given investment, you shouldn't be considering it at all.

● Risk, too, is largely a personal matter. You can take advice, and you will understand that investments that have high returns may well have a catch somewhere, but your preferences must decide the matter.

WORKING WITH METHOD

Investing your wealth has nothing to do with impulse or passing fancies. Any investment opportunity that apparently requires you to 'hurry along' is therefore to be avoided. It is most unlikely that you will miss anything worthwhile if you take your time.

Running with routine

Routine is your friend! Your money deserves care and attention, not rough-and-ready treatment, and doing everything by the book – your book – is the best way of making sure that you stay in control. While you may have to start off by constantly referring to your notes or even this book itself, you will find that after a time you run through the various checks and calculations almost automatically.

Successful money management demands two sorts of routine, both of which have been mentioned under different headings:

1. Routine that tells you **where you are**: this includes your periodical mark-to-market exercise and tracking your income and spending.

2. Routine that tells you **where to go**: this means the methodical application of the three investment principles when you invest your money.

Avoiding emotion

Routine also helps to keep you objective about your investments. You must always bear in mind the fact that money is not human! It will not be offended if you pick one form of investment over another. Nor will it laugh at you if you sell an investment before its intended maturity because it isn't performing as well as it should. These points sound trivial enough. But rest assured that there are plenty of investors out there who stick to unprofitable assets as if doing anything else would mean a loss of face.

Emotion can creep unbidden into what look like methodical calculations, too. Take expected return. Since it is up to you to estimate it, what is going to stop you giving the highest return to the share that was your favourite (for some trivial or illogical reason) all along?

The answer, of course, is that there is *nothing* that will stop you doing this! Your only protection is your own self-discipline and sense of reason. Nobody can stop you putting your money on a horse in the Grand National because it has a funny name, not if you're set on it. But what was said about magic in Chapter 7 holds true here too: be emotional if you want to, but keep your money out of it!

CALLING THE SHOTS

This round-up of what has been covered so far would be incomplete if we passed over your qualifications to manage your own money. There is a tendency to lose confidence in the face of the fact that there are all manner of investment experts out there. Furthermore, many of them seem willing and able to grapple with various assets on your behalf.

This is not a positive mind-set. Imagine purchasing an old house that requires renovation. Even if you had the money, would you call in an architect and interior designer, and say. 'Do what you like. Let me know when you're finished'? Yet this is *exactly* what handing your money over to an adviser involves!

The point is this. Being in control does *not* mean that you have to be an expert yourself. As with the house, the experts are there to give you their opinions when you want them, but it is up to *you* to make the final decision.

Controlling in practice

Several practical steps to keep you in the driving-seat were explored in the previous chapter. Don't let them slip from your mind:

● When you're listening to expert advice, take notes. Distinguish between facts and opinions, and don't bother writing down anything that sounds muddled or confusing. People who can't explain what they mean often don't know what they mean.

● Ask questions, no matter how basic. The simplest questions are often the most difficult to answer.

● Never make an investment decision without taking the time to think about it *on your own*. If an adviser is pressing you for an answer, too bad. Make an appointment for a future meeting or phone call.

● Don't be afraid to double-check investment advice.

SUMMARY

1. While attention has to be paid to the detail, it is important to see how it all fits together.

2. You can't manage your wealth at all unless you know both how much you have and whether what you have is increasing or decreasing every month.

3. It is suggested that you keep a monthly record of your mark-to-market as well as your income and spending.

4. Your monthly record should be properly written down, as should your investment guidelines.

5. Your guidelines serve as a screening device to stop you wasting your time analysing unsuitable investments.

6. Possible investments that survive screening by your guidelines may be assessed using the three investment principles: maturity, expected return and risk.

7. Your opinions can't be kept out of the investment principles. Don't be afraid of them.

8. Methodical treatment of your money in general, and possible investments in particular, makes it less likely that you will be hurried into something inappropriate or wildly emotional.

9. Being in control of your money does not mean that you have to be an expert yourself.

10. When listening to advice, take notes, ask questions, take your time, and double-check where you are in doubt.

POINTS TO CONSIDER

1. Do big city department stores have New Year sales because they want to be nice to you? Do they mind having lots of shoppers rushing down the aisles at opening time? Why do television advertisements tell you to 'Call now' and 'Hurry'?

2. What use is a map and compass if you don't know where you are?

3. Do bookmakers look forward to the Grand National?

9

Speaking Financially

BANKING ON DEPOSITS

Just about everyone in Britain has a bank (or building society) account of some sort, so it may seem odd at first to think of your money in the bank as an investment. But this money is part of your wealth and it is available to be managed. And the three investment principles work as well with bank accounts as they do with any other assets.

Running through your options

You do not need to spend long in your local bank or building society to realise that there are a wide variety of refuges for your money. Some accounts may have catchy names, but they usually boil down to one of the following:

- **Current accounts** give you instant access to your money and may or may not pay interest. If they do pay interest, the interest rate will normally be lower than that for a deposit account and will vary over time. You should reserve this type of account for your current spending needs (remember Chapter 1).

- **Deposit accounts** pay interest. The interest rate will vary over time and will usually be higher for larger deposits than for small ones. Access to your money may also be restricted. Your money can stay in the account for as long as you wish.

- **Fixed-term** (or simply **term**) **deposits** are deposits where you tie up your money for a specified length of time. This is usually expressed in a number of months (one, two, three, six and twelve months are common). You cannot withdraw your money before the 'term' has expired without incurring a charge of some sort. What you gain is an interest rate that is often higher than that on other sorts of bank deposits. When the term is up you may either make a new deposit of this type or have your money returned to a current or deposit account.

Applying investment principles

Bank accounts pose few difficulties when you come to apply the three investment principles to them. However, there are a few points that need some care:

- Remember that there are no stated **maturities** for bank accounts, apart from fixed-term deposits. It is up to you to assign a maturity, especially if you are comparing the attractiveness of a bank account against something else. If you wish to invest for three years, for example, and are comparing a deposit account with a savings bond (see below), **make sure you calculate your expected return on the basis of three years for the deposit account** as well as expected return for the bond.

- In Chapter 4 we talked about **yield curves**. Turn back to that section and then think about fixed-term deposits. Is there anything in there that could help you decide what maturity (term) of deposit to go for?

- The **interest rates** that banks will quote you for all interest-bearing accounts are usually so many per cent per year. However, if you multiply the interest rate by the size of your deposit, you may arrive at a slightly different figure (in pounds and pence) for your annual interest than will the bank. This is because the banking system uses standard '**day-counts**' for its interest calculations. Because months and years have different numbers of days, the system finds it convenient to pretend that each month and year have the same number of days for interest calculation purposes. It isn't a rip-off! Suffice to say that **over time you should not gain or lose from this system**. Just be aware that it exists.

- The **risk** of a bank account is that of the bank itself. If the bank collapses, you may not recover your money – as was the case for depositors at the Bank of Credit and Commerce International (BCCI) in 1991. Beware of smaller banks that offer especially high interest to depositors.

LOCKING IT UP: SAVINGS BONDS

A savings bond works in the same way as a fixed-term deposit. By buying a bond you lock up your money for a set length of time (the maturity is fixed), and taking your money out early will have a financial penalty. In return you expect to receive higher interest than you could get if your money were kept readily available. There are three possible differences between savings bonds and fixed-term deposits:

1. Banks are not the only institutions that offer savings bonds. The obvious example is that of National Savings bonds, which are issued by a government agency (National Savings) and are advertised in post offices.

2. Some savings bonds are transferable. You may buy them and give them to other people.

3. Savings bonds usually tie up your money for longer than fixed-term bank deposits. Their typical maturities are three or five years.

Applying investment principles

Much of what was said about bank deposits could be repeated for savings bonds. There are a few specific considerations, however:

●   There is a conspicuous exception to the rule that savings bonds have fixed maturities and interest rates. **Premium Bonds** have no maturity and no set interest rate. The interest is highly variable depending on whether 'your numbers come up' or not. Since expected return is entirely a matter of chance, Premium Bonds are impossible to compare with other investments. If you wish to hold these bonds, the best thing to do is to assume that they will return you nothing at all. You can only gain from there!

●   **National Savings bonds** are backed by the UK government. This is to say that in terms of the risk that you will lose your investment, these investments are about **as safe as they ever get**. They are even safer than deposits held at major banks.

PLAYING THE STOCK MARKET

The stock market is possibly the first thing that comes to mind when you dwell on possible investments. While it is far from true that it is the only financial investment you can make, it presents opportunities for increasing your wealth that many others cannot hope to compete with. But, as always, there's a catch…

Buying bits of companies

Shares are so-called because when you buy them you buy a share in a company. You become a part-owner of that company, no matter how small your shareholding. As a part-owner, you receive a share of the company's profits – **dividends** – and stand to gain or lose if the value of the company changes.

The stock market is where the shares of large companies are bought and sold. You can also buy shares (and then sell them) on the stock market, although you will need to pass your order through a stockbroker. This may be done for you by your bank or a share shop, or you may wish to approach a stockbroker directly. Whichever you choose, you will normally have to pay a commission.

The process of buying shares is actually very easy, so long as you know precisely which shares you wish to buy (or sell) and how much you are prepared to invest. You may specify the price at which you are willing to buy (sell) or you may leave it to the 'best efforts' of the stockbroker.

Putting it all on the table

As stated in the Preface, this book is not a list of all possible investments. Nor is it a guide to which shares you should or should not buy. Some such guides may be found in the 'Further reading' section at the end of this book. But this book *is* concerned with making investment decisions, and before you approach the stock market at all, you should be aware of two very important facts:

1. When you buy a share in a company, you stand to lose all your investment – t**he principal** – if the company goes bankrupt. As the advertisements say, 'The value of your investment may go down as well as up'. And 'go down' may mean that it falls to zero.

2. If the market decides that shares are not worth what they were, they will sell them, and share prices will fall. And if they feel that companies are worth more than share prices are telling them, they will buy shares, and prices will rise. **Note that your opinion or the 'facts' need not have anything to do with it.** It will be no good getting all frustrated when the price of your shares is falling, saying 'The market is mad!' because the price is what the market says it is, mad or not.

If you are set on buying shares, do consider professional management (see below).

Applying investment principles

Shares are special in more ways than one. Each investment principle needs to be applied carefully:

● You must stick to your **maturity**. If you buy shares as a six-month investment, you should not be still holding them after that time unless your priorities change. What often happens is that the share price does not get to where you thought it would be when the planned sale time arrives, and you 'give it a few more days'. The 'few more days' is liable to turn into weeks and then months, and meantime your money is tied up in an unplanned and probably hopeless investment.

● The **expected return** on a shareholding, as we saw in Chapter 6, has two elements: change in underlying value and investment income. The first is nothing other than the change in the share price, while the second consists of any dividends you will receive. Neither of them can be predicted with any certainly, although there are books that can help you arrive at a decent prediction (see 'Further reading').

● The **risk** of a share is the risk that the company does badly, either because it has internal problems or because it is engaged in a difficult business. You may have risk rules (see Chapter 2) that keep you off anything to do with activities you consider too risky for your money – this is precisely the sort of context where they would apply.

FUNDING THE GOVERNMENT

From time to time the government borrows money. Curiously enough, it borrows off people like you and me, either directly or indirectly. It either does so for reasons of economic policy or because it dares not raise taxes to pay for what it is spending; at times the sums involved have been very large indeed.

It borrows by issuing bonds, which are known as **Gilts** in financial markets. These are basically IOUs that almost always have a stated maturity and which pay interest (usually every six months).

Since Gilts may be sold before they mature, they are traded on the Stock Exchange in almost the same way as shares are. Their prices change daily, reflecting the market's view of how the government is managing its financial affairs and the British economy. You may buy them, either holding them to maturity (when the government pays back what it has borrowed) or selling them before they mature in the same way as you sell shares.

Gilts are not the only sorts of bonds that are traded on financial markets, but they are probably of most interest to individual investors.

Note that **bonds** are not the same as **savings bonds**. The latter are not traded on financial markets at all.

Coupon, price and face value

Gilts are more complicated than shares. The interest they pay is at a rate known as the **coupon**, which is fixed from the outset (with one exception, see below). This coupon is paid on the **face value** of the Gilt, usually £100. The face value is the amount the government will pay back at the Gilt's maturity date.

If you look at a list of Gilt prices (in the *Financial Times*, for example), it may strike you as odd that people are still interested in Gilts that bear coupons of, say, 6.25 per cent (a Gilt that matures in 2010), when there are Gilts that pay more, even for roughly the same maturity (there is a Gilt maturing in 2011 with a coupon of 9 per cent).

This is readily understandable when you recall that Gilt **prices** change. There is nothing preventing the price of a Gilt departing from its face value, although as maturity approaches they will gradually return to that value. A high-coupon Gilt will have a higher price than a low-coupon Gilt of the same maturity, which means that your effective return on investment will be the same. Figure 8 shows how coupon, price and face value operate for a hypothetical Gilt investment.

Gilt yields: a note for the very curious
The financial markets express the return on a Gilt as a yield. Their approach is unnecessarily complicated for the non-professional investor. However, if you are wondering what the yield figures used in the *Financial Times* are all about, here is the answer. The calculations start off much as shown in Figure 8, but three adjustments are made:

- it is assumed that interest income is used to buy more of the same Gilt

- the change in underlying value between purchase and maturity is calculated as if it happened today (using a 'present-value calculation', if mathematics is your thing)

- investment income and change in underlying value are lumped together and shown as an annual return (a percentage).

You will find Gilt yields useful if you wish to construct a yield curve for Gilts (see Chapter 4), but take **great care** in comparing yields with expected returns as calculated according to the method used in this book. You will not be comparing exactly the same thing.

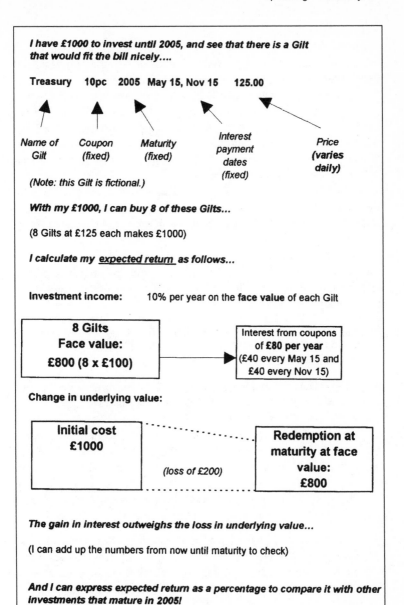

I have £1000 to invest until 2005, and see that there is a Gilt that would fit the bill nicely....

Treasury   10pc   2005   May 15, Nov 15   125.00

| Name of Gilt | Coupon (fixed) | Maturity (fixed) | Interest payment dates (fixed) | Price (varies daily) |

(Note: this Gilt is fictional.)

With my £1000, I can buy 8 of these Gilts...

(8 Gilts at £125 each makes £1000)

I calculate my <u>expected return</u> **as follows...**

Investment income: 10% per year on the **face value** of each Gilt

| **8 Gilts**
Face value:
£800 (8 x £100) | → | Interest from coupons of **£80 per year**
(£40 every May 15 and £40 every Nov 15) |

Change in underlying value:

| **Initial cost**
£1000 | | **Redemption at maturity at face value:**
£800 |

(loss of £200)

The gain in interest outweighs the loss in underlying value...

(I can add up the numbers from now until maturity to check)

And I can express expected return as a percentage to compare it with other investments that mature in 2005!

Fig. 8. A hypothetical Gilt investment.

Index-linked Gilts

These are Gilts that pay coupons that vary with the rate of inflation, with a fixed element to the coupon that is added to the change in the retail price index (RPI) to give you the overall coupon rate.

The attraction of these Gilts is that they give you total protection in the event that inflation rises. Inflation is not something we have really tackled yet – it appears in Chapter 11 – but you may have realised that there is no particular reason why the interest you receive on standard Gilts (and savings bonds and bank deposits, for that matter) should always be higher than the inflation rate.

This makes index-linked Gilts a very wise precaution if you believe that high inflation will return some day. Maturities on these Gilts extend to 2030, so you have a fairly long period in which to be proved right.

Applying investment principles

We've already touched on a few ways in which investment principles may be applied to Gilts. These plus a couple of others are summarised as follows:

- While the **maturity** of a Gilt is specified from the moment it is issued (except for a special class of Undated Gilts), there is nothing stopping you selling a Gilt long before its maturity date.

- The **expected return** on a standard Gilt is **known** from the moment you buy it, **if you hold that Gilt to its stated maturity**. This is why many professional investors find a place for Gilts somewhere in their portfolios. You know your investment income (the coupon, payable on every £100) and your change in underlying value (the difference between the price you pay, which depends on the market, and the redemption price at maturity, which is £100 per Gilt). However, if you plan to sell the Gilt before it matures you *will* have to estimate the change in underlying value.

- Gilts are backed by the financial weight of the British government. Like National Savings bonds, Gilts are as **risk-free** as investments ever get. No British government has ever failed to pay what it owes, either interest (coupons) or principal (redemption at maturity).

Buying Gilts

You may act through your bank or go directly to a stockbroker, as you would for a share purchase, or you can contact the National Savings Stock Register, which advertises in post offices.

You have a very wide choice of Gilt maturities. Indeed, there are Gilts that mature every year from the present year (they may have only weeks or months to run) to 2013, plus several that mature later still (2028 and 2030, for example). And there are a few that have no maturity date at all, called 'Undated', which are of limited interest to private individuals.

LEAVING IT TO OTHERS

Getting involved in financial markets need not mean that you have to go out and pick shares and Gilts all by yourself There are plenty of **fund managers** who will do the job for you. The ways they operate differ in certain respects, but they all take your money and invest it, often receiving a commission for doing so. You can usually withdraw your money without too much fuss, although, again, there may be some fee payable. There are pluses as well as minuses:

● **The pluses:**
   – you obtain the benefit of professional financial expertise
   – you need not follow the markets closely
   – fund managers operating in the UK are licensed and regulated
   – fund managers have to tell you how they performed in the past
   – you may have a wide choice of types of investment.

● **The minuses:**
   – the final investment decision passes from your hands
   – you may have to pay commissions
   – your own risk guidelines may not be respected
   – no fund manager can guarantee good future performance.

An idea that might appeal to you is to confer **part of your portfolio** on a fund manager, leaving the rest to your personal care. A comparison of how well the fund manager performs with how well you do on your own could prove most instructive. And not necessarily to the fund manager's credit!

Choosing a fund
There are hundreds of financial institutions that manage money on behalf of other people. A distinction should be made between **investment trusts** and **unit trusts**. **Stockbrokers** will also manage your money on a discretionary basis, provided you have the sort of funds to invest that justify their attention.

Investment trusts
Investment trusts are companies, and have shares that you can buy and

sell on the Stock Exchange. In that respect they are just like Boots and British Telecom. Their business, however, is to trade on financial markets, even using borrowed money to do so if they wish. The profits investment trusts make are distributed to shareholders, as for other companies. Some investment trusts specialise in generating investment income, while others go for capital growth (i.e. positive changes in underlying value). There are tax limits on how much money you can invest in investment trusts.

Unit trusts
Unit trusts simply manage investors' funds. The money they receive from ordinary investors is used to buy the shares, Gilts and even property that *they* feel to be good value. You invest your money by buying **units** in a fund; the better the find does, the higher the price of the unit. If all goes well, you sell your units for a profit at a time of your own choosing.

The various funds – and there are thousands of them – are run by companies that may or may not be subsidiaries of major banks. They are often distinguished by the sort of asset they invest in. The *FT Managed Fund Service* pages in the *Financial Times* give a startling insight into the range of investments unit trusts can offer (as well as contact telephone numbers and websites).

Selection criteria

Selecting a fund manager is a daunting task. You can go about it in three ways:

1. Decide the type of investment you want (shares, bonds, other) and the country you are interested in (it need not be the UK!), buy the *Financial Times*, and contact a range of unit trusts that offer what you want. Don't be put off by their high-flown names! They are used to dealing with people like you and me and will be delighted to send you further information on what they do.

2. Research the past and current performance of different funds. There are several magazines and websites that will give you this information (see 'Further reading'). Even though you know that last year's winner may be this year's loser, some funds do consistently well.

3. Ask the advice of your bank manager or stockbroker (if you use one). Be aware that banks and stockbrokers often have subsidiaries that run unit trusts, however. Make sure they suggest more than just their own people!

Applying investment principles

Investing in investment trusts and unit trusts should be treated in **exactly the same way** as a direct share investment, even if the trust is not invested in shares. They do not mature by themselves, are more or less risky, and it is up to you to evaluate future performance in terms of expected return.

STRIDING THE WORLD STAGE

Financially speaking, Britain is not an island. There is no reason why you should confine yourself to British financial investments, especially if you feel that some other part of the world is capable of generating high returns on your money.

Before you start researching investments abroad, take the time to find the answers to the following questions:

- Are there **exchange controls** in force, preventing your money from leaving the country in which you invest? Many countries are happy to see sterling coming in, but they won't let you take it away.

- Will you be liable to **local taxation** on your investments? If so, how much are you likely to have to pay?

- Have you taken **translation risk** (Chapter 3) into account?

You may well find that this 'pre-research' requires more information than you can get hold of. If this is the case, you are strongly advised to invest abroad via the intermediary of a unit trust. As we have seen, many unit trusts will invest your money in distant parts of the world for you and will take care of local regulations and taxes. They will not necessarily free you of translation risk, however. Ask them!

SUMMARY

1. Money in the bank is an investment like any other, and may be analysed using investment principles.

2. Although bank accounts can have a variety of names, they usually boil down to current accounts, deposit accounts and fixed-term deposits.

3. The risk of a bank account is the risk that the bank will collapse. Occasionally, banks do just that.

4. Savings bonds are an interesting alternative to fixed-term bank deposits.

5. Share investments may cost you part or all of your principal.

6. Share prices are decided by the market. If the price of a share you own seems crazy to you, too bad.

7. UK government bonds are known as Gilts. You can buy them in the same way as shares.

8. You should understand the difference between coupon, price and face value before you buy Gilts.

9. Fund managers invest on the world's financial markets on behalf of other people. If they do well on your behalf, you will benefit, but you may have to pay them fees.

10. If you want to invest in financial assets abroad, you are strongly advised to do so via the intermediary of a unit trust.

POINTS TO CONSIDER

1. When stock markets rise, do all share prices rise at the same rate? If not, why not?

2. If the government cuts taxes but cannot trim public expenditure, what do you think will happen to Gilt prices? Will new investors receive higher or lower returns on the Gilts they buy?

3. The government is not the only issuer of bonds. Major companies and banks issue bonds too. Assuming identical maturities, would you expect the return on a UK government bond (i.e. a Gilt) to be higher or lower than that on a bond issued by a major company?

10

Tackling the Tangible

PUTTING IT INTO PROPERTY

The British are rather unusual in that most of them – or members of their immediate family – own the places they live in (having a mortgage does *not* change that fact!). In most other countries rented accommodation is far more common. As a result, one could say that the British are a nation of property experts. Terms such as 'Stamp Duty' and 'planning permission' are widely understood in a way that 'coupon' and 'index-linked Gilt' never will be. It makes it all the more strange that investment in property – the family home aside – is not the first thing that springs to mind when money becomes available for investment. Why shy away from what is already fairly familiar to you?

Ticking off alternatives

The property market is divided into two parts, the **residential** sector and the **commercial** sector. This distinction is not made for the sake of it, but because price trends are often very different in each sector. Rising house prices do not necessarily mean rising rents for office premises, and vice versa. There is no reason why you shouldn't consider investing in commercial property, but don't base your calculations on some 'strong feeling' you may have on house prices.

That warning aside, you have three alternatives for property investment:

1. If you own your own home and include it as part of your wealth available to be managed (i.e. you would sell if the price was right, though not necessarily immediately), you could improve it. Whichever way you choose to do this, remember that this investment decision needs to make sense in the light of the three investment principles. Most pertinent of all, will the expected return be positive? In other words, will what you gain in the value of your property cover what you lose in improving it?

2. You could buy either residential or commercial property and let it, thus benefitting from investment income as well as any change in underlying value (price). The catch is that you either need plenty of

spare cash or need to be able to raise money from a bank or building society.

3. You could invest in a property-based investment trust or unit trust (see Chapter 9). The great advantage is that your investment need not be enormous: hundreds rather than thousands of pounds.

Applying investment principles

The three alternative investments listed above do not appear to have much in common. But when you look at them in the cold light of the investment principles, much the same questions appear in each case:

- Since property lasts for much longer than you do – barring hurricanes, wars and demolition orders – you have to set a **maturity** for your investment, even though it will probably have to be a fairly long one. This means having a good idea of when you will sell. As with shares, there is a tendency to hang on that little bit extra to give prices a chance to rise, and that situation is best avoided.

- The **expected return** on a property investment always includes change in underlying value (price rises or falls), and to that may or may not be added investment income (rent). It will not be news to you that there are costs involved in owning property, from taxes to maintenance, and even if you invest through a unit trust there are the inevitable commissions. Don't forget to factor in any mortgage or loan interest where these apply.

- While the property market has been a solid performer in the long run (60 million people crammed onto a small island have to hide from the rain *somewhere*), prices and rents can move very sharply from year to year. This is where most of your **risk** lies. Every time house prices fall, there are those who find that the value of their property is less than the loan they took out to buy it. The same thing happens – sometimes on a grand scale – in commercial property. You can't stop house prices falling, but nobody is forcing you to borrow excessive amounts either. If you want a flutter, put a pound on the horses. Not £80,000 you don't have on an overpriced house.

This section began with a question: 'Why shy away from what is already fairly familiar to you?' One answer would be as follows: 'Look, I own my own home, and I've got a large mortgage to pay off one day. I am therefore heavily involved in the property market as I stand. Why would I want to get involved even more?'

It's a point you *must* consider. It might even be covered by your risk rules (Chapter 2). If you're over-extended already, don't stretch any further!

TOUCHING ON GOLD

Of all the forms of wealth that are currently accepted throughout the world, gold must be the oldest. It is included here rather than in the chapter on financial assets because it predates financial systems by a very long way, and perhaps it will antedate them too!

Gold is reassuringly immune from hypothetical global computer collapses and the thousand and one calamities that can cripple economic life. When all else fails, from banks to shares to property prices, gold will still buy you food and shelter. It even works during the biggest human catastrophe of all, war.

Believing in doom

You don't have to believe in doom to want to buy gold, but pessimism never hurt gold prices! Every time the world economy does rather well for itself, gold is written off and prices decline. **This is why gold is being written off now.** Stock markets are performing strongly, save for the odd glitch, and even central banks are deciding they need not hold as many gold reserves as they used to. But it's funny how gold raises its head when things start to go wrong, as it has done for at least 6,000 years...

Buying gold

Gold you invest in comes in three basic forms:

1. Jewellery. This is *not* recommended for investment purposes, because jewellery is rarely made with pure gold, which is very soft, and because the value of gold jewellery is heavily affected by factors other than gold prices.

2. Gold coins (sovereigns and krugerrands, for example) and bars, which you can buy at gold merchants. The largest and most reputable merchants – you may find them under 'Bullion dealers' in the *Yellow Pages* – will normally be happy to advise you on the advantages and disadvantages of the various coins and bars available.

3. Gold shares or unit trusts. Here you do not buy gold directly, but invest in companies that mine it (shares) or finds that buy it for you and other investors (unit trusts). Refer back to Chapter 9 if this is the route you wish to take.

The catches

There are two major catches with buying gold: tax and translation risk. **Tax** is a problem with the first two alternatives listed above, since jewellery and gold purchases are subject to VAT at the full rate. That will certainly have a big impact on your expected return calculations. VAT can be avoided if you opt for second-hand jewellery, coins and bars, but you need to ensure that the gold is in pristine condition.

Translation risk (see Chapter 3) is present because gold is traditionally priced in US dollars. When you buy or sell gold in the UK, the dollar price is converted to pounds sterling for your convenience. If the dollar moves against you between the time you buy and the time you sell, too bad for you. It might move in your favour, of course, but give the issue some thought.

Applying investment principles

Even more so than property, gold lasts. **Maturity** will be up to you, but as always, you must respect that maturity, whether you have been proved right about prices or not. As for the other two principles, the following points are relevant:

● Gold does not produce investment income, although investing via the stock market (gold shares and unit trusts) can do. That aside, **expected return** consists entirely in the change in underlying value, i.e. gold prices. Be aware that gold prices have generally been *falling* for two decades, from around $850 per Troy ounce (the unit of measurement for gold, a little heavier than a normal ounce) in 1980 to around $300 in early 1999. Lastly, don't forget to factor in VAT if this applies.

● Gold will outlive life on this planet. The only **risks** you face, other than prices falling further still, are translation risk and getting it stolen...

DABBLING IN ART

The art market, like art itself, isn't reserved for millionaires. But investing in art – buying it with a view to selling it in the future – requires considerable expertise if it is to be successful. Liking art is not enough! To a knowledge of art history and the technical business of restoring and conserving art works needs to be added an eye for what is fashionable and what is not. At the very least, this means keeping up to date with sale prices.

If you are an expert in art, or at least some little bit of the art world, you will need no guidance from this book on what you can buy and how you go about buying it. But investment principles work just as well here as they do for other investments:

- The **maturity** you assign to a work of art isn't necessarily arbitrary. Many works – and not just paintings – require professional attention from time to time to stop them deteriorating. The length of time a work is in peak saleable condition may be limited.

- The **expected return** on works of art, as with gold coins, consists only of change in underlying value. Your estimate of what that will be will have to be adjusted for any taxes and commissions you will have to pay, as well as any storage and insurance costs for the work itself.

- Aside from being very disappointed by what art prices do, your principal **risk** lies in the physical loss or destruction of your art collection. Fortunately, you can normally insure against these events.

Perhaps more than most investment assets, art works grow on you. Even the shrewdest investor in the art market can fall prey to sentiment, and decide that a work already bought will not be sold at its designated maturity after all. If this happens to you, remove it from your list of assets available to be managed. It is either an investment or it isn't.

COLLECTING FOR PROFIT

Enthusiasm for collecting things can pass from occasional hobby to a serious occupation. Experts in stamps, fine china, antique furniture and Roman coins usually started off with little more than curiosity. And all but a few remain strictly amateur.

If you have a collector's eye and expertise to match, it may have occurred to you that there is money to be made by buying certain items, holding them for a while, and then selling them to other collectors or the professional trade. As we saw with works of art, so long as you are strict about what you are buying for investment purposes and what you are buying for yourself, there is no reason why putting your money to work in this way cannot succeed.

The three investment principles apply in the same way as they do for works of art.

WRITING OFF CARS

Cars were mentioned as early as Chapter 2. As you may recall, they were included as the classic example of a depreciating asset. People who buy cars do so because they find that their usefulness outweighs the persistent loss of their value. In our investment terminology, we say that **the expected return on a car is almost always negative**. As there is no investment income from a car (taxis aside), the loss in underlying value accounts for the entire expected return calculation.

Drawing up depreciation

Take a look at Figure 9. It shows what happens to the value of certain car models as they age. Just about all cars lose value from the moment they leave the showroom. They often pass through the hands of several owners before being sold for scrap. Scrapping occurs when the car's underlying value is lower than that of its metal content and used components.

As Figure 9 shows, however, some cars actually climb in value after a certain point. These, of course, are the collectors' items. Before you even consider making money out of them, ask yourself whether you have enough of what it takes in two fundamental areas:

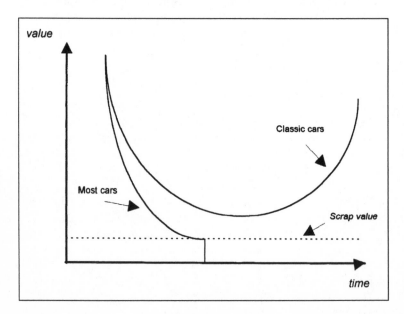

Fig. 9. What happens to cars.

1. **Mechanics.** This applies whether you intend to maintain the car personally or will pay someone else to do it. You need to know the nuts and bolts even if you're not going to spend all your time physically handling them.

2. **Market insight.** It may be obvious *now* which 1960s cars turned out to be collectors' items, but rest assured that it wasn't evident when they were new. Even if you do not propose to guess which current cars will be the classics of the future, intending to buy a car that is a classic already, you can't do without a firm idea of where the market is heading. Just because you like the car, it doesn't mean that everyone else will in five years' time.

Applying investment principles

These should be becoming familiar to you now! And so must be the principle that you need to be dispassionate while using them.

● As with all investments that do not come with **maturity** dates attached, you have to come up with one yourself *and stick to it.* Don't cling on to investments beyond the maturity dates you give them.

● The **expected return** on an investment in a car, as has been pointed out already, is almost always entirely composed of change in underlying value. And if the car does *not* become a classic the change in underlying value is persistently negative. Don't forget to include costs of spare parts, taxes, insurance and labour in any expected return calculation you do.

● As with an investment in shares, your entire **principal** may dwindle to something close to zero if you get the investment decision wrong. This is your main **risk.** Added to that are risks common to all assets that can 'walk', plus the particular concern that spare parts may become unobtainable or prohibitively expensive.

SUMMARY

1. Britain could be called a nation of property experts. If you have strong views about property prices or rents, you could make money out of those views.

2. Investing in property doesn't necessarily mean buying it. You could improve your own home or buy property-based unit trusts.

3. If you're over-extended on the property market already, don't stretch any further.

4. Gold is an unfashionable and unprofitable investment, as it always is when the world economy is doing reasonably well and the human race is reasonably secure from self-destruction. Investing in gold therefore presupposes a certain pessimism about the future.

5. As with property, investment in gold does not have to mean a direct purchase of the physical material. Gold shares and unit trusts can also give you the benefit of a rise in gold prices, as well as investment income.

6. Investment principles work just as well for purchases of works of art as they do for other forms of investment.

7. If a work of art bought for investment purposes grows on you, and you decide not to sell it at its maturity date, remove it from your list of investments to be managed and cease marking it to market.

8. If you collect items that have value (or will have value, in your opinion), don't be afraid of putting your money to work in that area. So long as you are strict about what you are buying for investment purposes and what you are buying for yourself, there is no reason why this cannot work.

9. Before you even consider making money out of classic cars, ask yourself whether you really know enough about mechanics and the classic car market.

10. The entirety of your investment in a car will depreciate to zero if you pick a classic that isn't.

POINTS TO CONSIDER

1. If you were selling your house or flat, what would you do to spruce it up? Would you spend £5,000 on a professional renovation? If not, why not? How would an expected return calculation help you here?

2. Do you believe in insuring against bad times? Is there a case for an investment in gold even if prices keep falling? Is there a parallel with car ownership here?

3. How do antique dealers decide how much they are willing to pay for items in auctions? How might the approach of investors in antiques differ?

11

Following the Markets

HUNTING FOR INFORMATION

You cannot manage your own money successfully if you do not have access to market prices and reports. This no-exception rule covers *every* investment you make, financial or non-financial. There are five good uses of this information:

1. You will remember from Chapters 1 and 2 that you cannot even begin to move forward until you know where you are. You need to **mark-to-market** all those assets you already own that are available to be managed. How can you do this without prices?

2. You are most unlikely to come up with credible estimates of **expected return** for a possible investment if you ignore all that has happened to that type of investment in the past. While past performance is absolutely no guarantee of the future, you would be wrong to ignore it completely.

3. You are not going to make an investment decision and then walk away from it. Apart from telling you where you are, marking-to-market as you progress tells you how well your investments are doing. They therefore enable you to monitor your own **performance**.

4. Market events and news may give you **early warning of poor performance** to come, giving you a chance to change your mind (see Chapter 12).

5. Tracking the markets that interest you will make you a wiser investor. It won't stop you getting predictions wrong, but it will give you a **better feel for how markets operate** (again, see Chapter 12). One day it may keep you out of big trouble.

Finding your sources

Depending on the type of investment, you may need to do some spadework. Some markets (especially financial markets) are obliged by law to publish information on prices and transactions; many others are almost secretive in this regard. Make sure you exhaust all possible sources of information before you give up on an investment that appeals to you.

The trade press

These days there is a 'trade' press for just about any investment. The financial world has a very old trade press, of course, headed by the unbeatable *Financial Times*. But investments from fine English shotguns to first edition books and property to art have also spawned specialist magazines and newspapers.

Libraries

Libraries are good sources of both background information and market prices. They often stock reference books that are prohibitively expensive for most pockets, especially annual statistical digests.

The internet

If you already use the Internet, you will appreciate just how much information is available to you. The problem is rather that there is too much, and you may find that the trade press is still worth your attention. It may well list appropriate websites, which certainly saves time on-line. A handful of websites are listed in 'Further reading'; treat these only as a start.

If you do not have access to the internet, try it (at a friend's or at certain libraries, for instance) before you even think of buying it. It may well be that you can get the information you seek more easily and more cheaply elsewhere.

Weighing up commentary

As you may have already noticed, there is more to market information than simply prices. There is commentary, too. Every market has its experts, and experts have opinions that are aired in the trade press and elsewhere. In Chapter 7 you were encouraged to sift fact from opinion when listening to expert advice; the same care applies to reading it, too. Opinion is a valuable complement to fact, but only if you recognise it as such.

Deciding who is talking sense and who isn't is a matter for your own judgement. One pointer that has mentioned before may help you here. **Confusing or garbled commentary is usually a sign of confused and garbled thinking.** If you can't follow it, it doesn't mean that you are thick. It means that the writer hasn't got it straight in his or her own mind.

CHECKING PERFORMANCE

Part of the reason for following the markets is monitoring the performance of your investments. This means measuring how well they are doing (i.e. what their return is actually turning out to be) against certain standards. Whatever standards you use to measure your performance, they should always include **expected return**. Other suggested standards would be your own **performance objectives** (if you have any).

Comparing actual and expected return

Expected return is undoubtedly the most subjective of the three investment principles. Once you have made your investment decision, however, the return on that investment tends to become less subjective as time goes by. At maturity, of course, there is no more 'expected' about it.

A comparison example
Imagine that you choose to invest in some unit trusts for a two-year period. You have compared these unit trusts with other investments, and the former win the day because you expect them to return **20 per cent** between now and maturity, even taking costs and taxes into account. You have assumed that there is no investment income, reasoning that any you do receive will be a bonus. Thus the entire 20 per cent return is made up of change in underlying value.

Once the investment is made, the unit trust investment passes onto that list of assets that you mark to market every month. You note that after six months the underlying value of this investment (i.e. the price multiplied by the number of units you own) has risen by 3 per cent. How well is this asset performing? Is it meeting your expectations or not?

The fact that six months have elapsed does *not* mean that you can say what will happen in the other 18 months. But you *can* say that if your units continue to rise *at the same rate rate* as their actual return so far – 3 per cent every six months – they will end up returning you **12.6 per cent** after two years. You can say that so far the investment is *not* performing as expected. You may want to think again…

If you can't see where 12.6 per cent came from, turn back to Chapter 5. Think **compounding**!

Performing against objectives

Back in Chapter 2 you were advised to set objectives for your investments. One of the examples given referred to the rate of inflation (you might want to increase your portfolio's value by more than the inflation rate each year), another referred to 'beating' the interest rate on a deposit account. Yet another, less ambitious, was at least to maintain the current value of your assets (i.e. avoid losing money). In each case, you would simply calculate the actual return on your portfolio from time to time (using your mark-to-market figures) and compare it with your objective, compounding if necessary.

QUESTIONS AND ANSWERS

What is inflation?
Inflation is the economic phenomenon of generally rising prices. Prices for the goods and services you buy have been rising for many decades, sometimes rapidly, and at other times almost too slowly for you to notice. There is no shortage of economic theories to explain why this happens, and there are some easily digestible books that can give you an insight into the problem (see 'Further reading'). For our purposes here, suffice to say that the rate at which prices rise is known as the rate of inflation.

UK inflation is measured in several ways. The most common measure is the **retail price index** or 'RPI', which is simply a measure of how prices of an imaginary 'basket' of everyday purchases move. If your investment objective consists of beating the RPI, this means that you intend to increase the value of your managed assets every year by at least the rise in the RPI. As the latter is always expressed as a percentage, it makes comparisons easy.

Why choose beating inflation as an investment objective?
Say the value of your portfolio increases by exactly the same rate as inflation (the RPI) over one year. This means that your assets can buy just as much at the end of that year as they could at the start of the year. Your assets are worth a little more, but prices have risen by the same amount, and you are no better or worse off. An economist would say that the **real value** of your portfolio is unchanged.

Now imagine that the value of your portfolio increases, but by not as much as the rate of inflation (for example, the portfolio gains 2 per cent in value, but the RPI rises 3 per cent). What does this mean? You cannot buy as much at the end of the year as you could at the beginning, even though the value of your portfolio has risen. An economist would say that your portfolio has **gained** in **current** value, but **lost** in **real** value.

Now you can see why trying to beat the rate of inflation is not such a bad plan. If the value of your portfolio increases faster than prices do, your **real wealth** will grow. You will indeed be able to buy more with your wealth (should you wish to spend it) at the end of each year than you could at the start.

Why beat the rate of interest on deposit accounts?
Those people who decide to do nothing with money they have available for investment typically leave it on deposit. It is an almost effortless thing to do, the money is usually safe enough, and it earns something. If you make the effort to try and do something constructive with your money, it will do you good to know that you are beating all those who can't be bothered!

What is a market benchmark?
This sort of objective, unlike the two mentioned above, is peculiar to financial investments. The performance of financial markets is often summarised in indices, and professional money managers will gauge their performance by referring to the appropriate index. The most well known financial index is probably the **FTSE 100**, which is used to generalise the performance of the UK stock market.

The FTSE 100 is the average price of shares in 100 very large companies, covering all types of business. Professionals who invest in shares will often try and beat the FTSE 100, which means that they try and do better than the market generally. If their portfolios gain 10 per cent in value over the year and the FTSE 100 rises 20 per cent, they are considered to have done badly. If the FTSE 100 falls 10 per cent, and the value of their portfolios is unchanged over the year, they are considered to have done rather well.

The FTSE 100 is not the only stock market index, even for the UK. The *Financial Times* lists many different stock market indices, many of which cover particular types of shares. Other financial markets have indices too, including bond (and therefore Gilt) markets, but they are far less well known to the general public.

AVOIDING THE AUTOMATIC RESPONSE

The point of monitoring the actual return on your investment as it unfolds is straightforward. If your estimate of expected return is turning out to be correct or pessimistic (actual return is shaping up higher than you'd supposed), all well and good. But if actual return is turning out to be rather disappointing, you might consider selling that investment early in favour of another. Figure 10 shows the difficult decision before you.

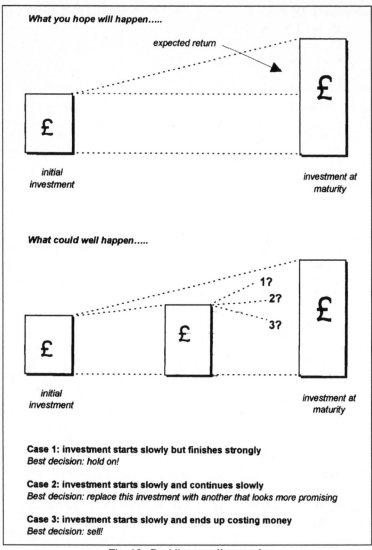

Fig. 10. Deciding to sell out early.

As you can see, the decision to sell should *not* be an automatic response to poor performance. This is because actual returns are not always even. A three-year investment in shares may look rather poor after the first year but go on to perform strongly in the second and third years. Selling investments as soon as they start to falter is hardly ever good policy. All investments have bad days, and if the plan is to keep them for months or years, you need to take those days in your stride.

Keeping your distance

There is clearly a bit of a balancing act here. If an investment is really going wrong, you would be better off without it; if it is merely stopping for a breather along its journey, selling would be a shame. How can you tell one situation from the other, though?

Well, you can't. If you could, you would be wildly rich already. Having said that, you can make sensible decisions on the matter. The key is **keeping your distance**. The closer you watch the markets, the more prone you will be to sell early. While you need to *follow* the markets (that much should be abundantly clear by now), a weekly or monthly check of how things are going will be more than enough for most investments.

The truth of the matter is that poor performance of an investment usually becomes evident over time. This means weeks or even months. 'Crashes' aside, you have time to think about what an investment is really doing. People who trade in financial markets, to take a spectacular example, buy and sell all day and change their minds frequently. **This is not a good guide for you!** They do it because they are trading very large amounts indeed – sometimes hundreds of millions of pounds – and the slightest move in the market makes a big difference to them. And slight moves are really not your concern.

SUMMARY

1. You cannot manage your own money successfully if you do not have access to market prices and reports.

2. Market information enables you to mark-to-market, to make good estimates of expected return and to monitor your performance. It may also provide early warning of difficulties ahead and will give you a better feel of how markets operate.

3. Make sure you exhaust all possible sources of information before you give upon an investment that appeals to you.

4. The trade press, libraries and the Internet are all good sources of market information.

5. Opinion is a valuable complement to fact, but only if you recognise it as such. Read market commentary, but use your discretion in deciding what makes sense.

6. You should always measure your performance against expected return. You might also measure it against your own performance objectives (if you have any).

7. If the value of your portfolio increases faster than prices do, your **real wealth** will grow.

8. The performance of financial markets is often summarised in indices, and professional money managers will gauge their performance by referring to an index.

9. The decision to sell an investment before its planned maturity should not be an automatic response to poor performance. Actual returns do not always progress evenly.

10. While you need to follow the markets, a weekly or monthly check of how things are going will be more than enough for most investments.

POINTS TO CONSIDER

1. Can you have a pay rise and a real cut in pay at the same time? Does a persistently rising market guarantee a real increase in your wealth invested in it?

2. Imagine that you have to make a long car journey. If you see a traffic jam ahead, do you immediately think of turning back to find another route? Is there a certain time that you will put up with the traffic jam before you think again? Does this help you understand the dilemma of selling investments early?

3. If you had to perform a mark-to-market every day, would it make you a better or worse investor? Can you see why one month was recommended as a mark-to-market interval?

12

Gaining in Confidence

IMPROVING WITH EXPERIENCE

Practice can't make perfect when it comes to investment, but it *can* make it better. No investor, amateur or professional, can tell you what will happen, but some consistently weather storms better than others. Some of it is connected with your character – the less emotional you are about your investment decisions, the better – but the rest has a lot to do with familiarity. This is especially true in three respects:

● gaining a feel for the market

● knowing who gives the best advice

● understanding warning signs.

Feeling the market
Every competent cyclist will know what 'getting a feel' for something means. As a fumbling beginner, events simply happen and it is all you can do to stay upright. It is not acting, but reacting. All of a sudden, and often after a bit of a bruising, you find that you 'sense' what you are doing in a new way. You are no longer fighting, but feeling. Your gestures become less exaggerated, use less energy, and are more effective.

Getting a feel for the market is a similar process. No matter what the investment, there are periods when prices rise, others when they fall. There may be particular points during the year when the market tends to move a lot, others when it is calm. Every market will react particularly strongly to some types of news and ignore others. The more you follow a market, the more you will understand and even anticipate these things.

Selecting advice
Strangely enough, bad advisers rarely wither away. Experts are rarely sacked when they are wrong, presumably because it is felt that they are bound to be right sooner or later and can 'talk a good book'. When you are new to a market (again, it could be silver spoons or Gilts) you have

no way of knowing who knows what is going on and who doesn't. The longer you follow markets, the clearer the identities of the real experts become.

Reading the signs

Not every storm comes with a warning, but many do. Signs that a market may be in for a bit of a bumpy time will not necessarily mean that you will want to bail out, but having a good idea of what could happen will do your confidence no harm at all. The sorts of warning signs you could encounter might include the following:

● prices rising well ahead of what you consider to be sustainable levels

● nervousness on the part of trusted experts

● newspaper comment (the daily papers, not the trade press) urging investors to get stuck in – often a sign that things are getting out of hand

● dwindling numbers of transactions, even though prices have not yet moved.

You will have noted that some of these warning signs are apparently good news, especially the first! Fast rising markets always stop somewhere. And the sensation is not always pleasant...

GETTING OUT IN A HURRY

In an ideal world you would choose investments that met your own criteria for risk and maturity and which presented an acceptable expected return, and that expectation would be met or exceeded. You would hold your investments until their planned maturity, and reap the rewards at your leisure.

Of course, it isn't always like that! The march of events may lead you to decide to change your plans. In the extreme case, it may appear imperative that you extricate yourself from your investments as soon as possible and hold your assets in the form of cash in a current account instead.

If it is only you that feels this urge, doing the deed presents no special problems. But if everyone feels as you do, getting out can be very tricky indeed. If everyone tries to sell, prices drop, and the more they drop, the more people want to get out. And so it goes on, until market prices are so low that buyers step in once again and calm things down.

Thinking, not running

You would do well to keep calm, even if you see your shares dropping in price by the hour. If you were comfortable with your investments before the selling started, do yourself a favour and **think** before you join the rush. Ask yourself the following questions:

● Is the reasoning that gave me my expected return numbers still intact?

● Had prices been rising more quickly than they really should have been?

● Would I regret not holding these investments when the fuss dies down?

If the answer to any of these questions is 'yes', don't run. If there is at least one 'no', however, you may indeed have to bite the bullet. But even at that stage, you should avoid trying to get out 'at any price'. 'Any' price will almost certainly be a bad one.

Keeping your wits about you

If things go wrong, and quickly, do try and keep some perspective on events. Panicking markets always exaggerate bad news, and all recover their nerve sooner or later. If your investment has years to run until its planned maturity, there may be no good reason why a crash in prices now cannot be made up with time to spare.

There was a striking example of a crash and a subsequent recovery in 1998. European and American stock markets all slumped alarmingly between the middle of July and the end of September. Most share prices dropped by **between 20 per cent and 30 per cent**, only to recover more or less all these losses by the end of November!

Your investments are going to be mainly long-term commitments, probably stretching over several years. You are therefore interested in **long-term** trends. Market crashes are **short-term** phenomena. A market crash may indeed be a symptom of a long-term malaise, but it isn't necessarily the case.

CONFESSING MISTAKES

Getting it wrong is part and parcel of investing money. Indeed, the difference between a successful investor and an unsuccessful one is not that one doesn't make mistakes and the other does. It is that the former learns from mistakes and can always move on.

Pretending that you have the Midas touch will do you no good. No matter how competent an investor you become, you are always going to make bad as well as good decisions. While dwelling on your errors all night is going too far, failed investments should always prompt the following questions:

● Am I systematically over-optimistic about my expected return calculations?

● Were there any warning signs that indicated the investment might go wrong? Was I blind to what I did not want to see?

● Did any experts predict what would happen?

● Do my risk rules need tightening?

Once you have given your mistakes this sort of examination, **move on**. Everyone has to take a smack in the face from time to time, in investment as in everything else they do.

SPREADING YOUR WINGS

As you improve as an investor, mistakes and successes all moving you on a little more, you will almost certainly ask yourself whether you should commit a higher proportion of your portfolio to riskier investments. This is a healthy process, and reflects your increased confidence.

Daring a little

Trying your hand at riskier investments may well involve relaxing some of your risk rules. There is absolutely nothing wrong with that, so long as taking on more risk is a reflection of your increased experience and confidence. If it is driven by a need to 'make up' for poorly performing investments, you should not consider such a move.

One approach that may appeal to you is the following. If your portfolio performs better than you had expected, you could commit the 'surplus' return to riskier investments. It would be a sort of reward for your shrewd management, and if you lost that surplus, well, you hadn't been banking on it anyway.

SLEEPING AT NIGHT

Taking control of your own money is a positive step. It is one way of asserting your control over your own affairs, and the fact that you can succeed, using your own experience and judgement, is good reason to hold your head high. If it gives you sleepless nights, however, and you constantly worry about what might happen to your money, you have missed the point somewhere.

Leaving your affairs to the experts is a sign of misplaced confidence. As we have seen, experts do not know the future any more than you do, and while you would do well to listen to what they say, your own considered judgement is nothing to be ashamed of. Would you let an expert vote for you? If not, why let them poke their fingers in your wallet?

Being in charge is nothing to be frightened of. Actually, it can be quite a lot of fun. You will be surprised at what you can do and what you can learn. It might even lift you in other parts of your life, too. And perhaps you will sleep better than ever.

SUMMARY

1. Investment will never be a science, and practice will never make your decisions perfect. It can, however, make them better.

2. Experience gives you a feel for the market, an appreciation of who gives the best advice, and helps you to read the warning signs.

3. Selling investments in a hurry presents no special problems if you are the only investor who wants to do it. But if everyone feels as you do, getting out can be very tricky indeed.

4. Panic is infectious, especially on financial markets. You will do well to keep calm.

5. Avoid trying to get out 'at any price'. 'Any' price will almost certainly be a bad one.

6. If things go wrong, and quickly, do try and keep some perspective on events. Panicking markets always exaggerate bad news, and all recover their nerve sooner or later.

7. The difference between a successful investor and an unsuccessful one is not that one doesn't make mistakes and the other does. It is that the former learns from mistakes and can always move on.

8. Relaxing some of your risk rules as you gain experience is a healthy process, so long as taking on more risk is a reflection of your increased experience and confidence and is not an attempt to make up for poor investments.

9. Taking control of your own money is a positive step. If it gives you sleepless nights you have missed the point somewhere.

10. You will be surprised at what you can do and what you can learn.

POINTS TO CONSIDER

1. Can you have a successful day out at the horse-racing if you get a couple of your selections wrong? Does this tell you anything about diversifying your investments?

2. What is the point of investing in riskier assets? How might you decide between two high-risk investments?

3. Imagine you have an investment (shares in a company, say) that is performing extremely well but which suddenly steps outside your risk limits (it proposes to buy another company that is involved in a far riskier business). What should you do: sell this investment before you planned to, or change your risk limits?

Glossary

Appreciation. The rise in the value of an asset.

Asset. A general term for something owned that has value.

Base currency. The currency that is worth 1 against a given amount of another currency.

Base rate. The rate at which the Bank of England will lend to the banking system. A change in this rate is a signal to banks in general that they should alter their lending and deposit rates too.

Bid/offer prices. The prices at which a professional dealer will buy from you and sell to you, respectively. The offer price will always be higher than the bid price.

Billion. Now universally accepted as 1,000 million.

Bond. An IOU issued by a company or a government that can be traded in the financial markets, usually, maturing after several years.

Compounding. The mathematical process of calculating interest on a sum that includes interest already received.

Coupon. The interest rate payable on a bond, expressed as a return on the bond's face value.

Crash. A dramatic slump in market prices, usually used in connection with shares and property.

Current spending. Spending that does not add to your wealth.

Depreciation. The fall in the value of an asset.

Dividend. Company profits distributed to shareholders, quoted as so many pence per share.

Euro. The common currency of eleven European countries. It has a fixed value against each of the eleven national currencies, and will be the sole currency of those countries from 2002.

Expected return. The total return you expect to receive from an investment.

Face value. The notional value of a bond. It is the value on which the coupon is paid (which may not be its market value) and the amount per bond the issuer will repay at maturity.

Foreign exchange. A general term for foreign currencies.

Gilt. A bond issued by the UK government, so-called because at one time the certificates proving ownership had gilded edges.

Income. An inflow of assets that will increase your wealth if it is not all lost as current spending.

Inflation. An economic phenomenon of a generally rising price level. Often measured with reference to the retail price index (RPI).

Interest. The income receivable from borrowers on the money they borrow. This includes bonds and bank deposits as well as straight loans.

Internet. A computer-based information network that uses telecommunications systems to transfer data.

Investment. A store of your wealth. It may be financial or non-financial in nature.

Investment income. Income that flows from ownership of an investment.

Investment trust. A company that makes its money by trading on financial markets. Profits are distributed to shareholders in the normal way.

Liquidity premium. The value placed on holding liquid assets. The higher this value, the more incentive is required to invest money for a long period.

Marking-to-market. The process of 'marking' every component of the wealth that you propose to manage with a 'market' price.

Maturity. The time at which the life of an asset will end (leaving you with your money to invest afresh) or at which you plan to sell the asset.

Maturity profile. The breakdown of a portfolio by maturity type (e.g. short-term assets, long-term assets).

Mortgage. A secured loan, widely used to finance house purchases. Failure to repay the interest or principal on the loan could mean the legal transfer of ownership of the assets put up as security to the creditor.

Portfolio. A group of assets regarded as one unit.

Redemption. The maturity of those assets (e.g. bonds) that have specific lifetimes.

Risk limits. Your own set of rules that limits the riskiness of your investments.

Risk rating. A risk 'score' given to an investment by a rating agency.

Savings bond. A bond issued by a bank or the government that carries a fixed rate of interest and which usually ties up the investor's money for several years. Aimed at individual savers, it is not traded on financial markets.

Shares. Part of the ownership of a company, entitling the holder to a share of the company's profits. The shares of public companies are traded on stock markets.

Spreadsheet. A computer programme suitable for storing numbers and performing calculations.

Stockbroker. A company or individual licensed to deal in shares and Gilts.

Stock market. The central point for all trading in shares in public companies. The UK stock market is named the Stock Exchange.

Stocks. A general term for shares and Gilts, often used mistakenly as a synonym for shares alone.

Translation risk. The risk that any gains on an investment denominated in a foreign currency are wiped out by changes in the value of the foreign currency against the pound.

Underlying value. The value of an asset were you to sell it. The change in underlying value is one possible part of the return on an investment (investment income is the other).

Unit trust. A fund which pools money from many investors and uses it to buy shares, Gilts and property. Investors buy one or several units which gain in value if the unit trust manages its funds profitably.

Wealth. A stock of assets, not to be confused with income.

Website. An internet address specific to a company, individual or other user that displays any information that the addressee wishes to make public.

Yield. The return on an investment given known maturity, investment income and price.

Further Reading

GENERAL INVESTMENT ADVICE

10 Steps to Financial Success, W. Patrick Naylor (Wiley, 1997).
Managing Your Personal Finances, John Claxton (How To Books, 1999).
The Investors Chronicle Personal Finance Planner, Debbie Harrison (Pitman, 1998).

FINANCIAL INVESTMENTS

Be Your Own Stockbroker, Charles Vintcent (Pitman, 1996).
Investing in Stocks & Shares, John White (How To Books, 1999).
The Armchair Investor, Bernice Cohen (Orion, 1997).
The Barron's Guide to Making Investment Decisions, Donald Jay Korn (New York Institute of Finance. 1993).
The Investors Chronicle Beginners Guide to Investment, Bernard Gray (Century Business, 1993).

NON-FINANCIAL INVESTMENTS

Buying and Selling Antiques, Sara Pitzer (Storey Communications, 1995).
Buying Classic and Vintage Cars for Profit, Tony Bosworth (Hale, 1996).
Coins and Investment, Andrew Moore (B. A. Seaby, 1986).
How to Make Money Out of Antiques, Judith Millar (Mitchell Beazley, 1995).

DIRECTORIES AND FINANCIAL TERMS

The CNBC Dictionary of Financial and Investing Terms, R. J. Shook (McGraw, 1996).
The Handbook of International Financial Terms, Peter Moles and Nicholas Terry (OUP, 1997).

The Investors Chronicle A–Z of Investment, Caroline Sefton (Pitman, 1996).

The Investors Chronicle Guide to Stockbrokers, Veronica McGrath (Pitman, 1996).

UNDERSTANDABLE ECONOMICS

The Illustrated Guide to the British Economy, Bill Jamieson (Duckworth, 1998).

The UK Economy, A. R. Prest (OUP, 1996).

WEBSITES

There are thousands upon thousands of websites dedicated to investing, especially in financial assets. Those listed below are especially helpful for the non-professional investor.

http://www.moneyworld.co.uk (glossary, comprehensive lists of stockbrokers, banks, other financial advisers, etc. plus background information)

http://ft.com (*FT* online, free)

http://www.bloomberg.com (financial news and data)

http://www.exchangeandmart.co.uk (every kind of non-financial asset you can imagine)

http://www.autotrader.co.uk (cars)

Index

PAYING OFF YOUR MORTGAGE
How to choose and change mortgage options to save money

Tony Cornell

How would you like to pay a mortgage off in half the time or less, without dramatically changing your lifestyle? If so, regardless of whether you currently have a mortgage or are looking for one, this informative book will teach you various mortgage reduction techniques and show you how to utilise a mortgage to your advantage. In so doing you could take years off the term, and save thousands of pounds. Written in jargon-free language the author explains everything from choosing the right lender, selecting and applying for the right mortgage, avoiding fees and charges, understanding interest rates, including the new Aussie rules method, and much more besides. Tony Cornell is a self-employed finance consultant with over ten years' experience as a licensed mortgage broker.

114pp. illus. 1 85703 396 5.

ARRANGING INSURANCE
How to manage policies and claims for everyday personal and business purposes

Terry Hallett

This book provides a step-by-step guide explaining in simple terms what to do when a mishap is suffered in the home, and how to pursue a successful insurance claim. It is written by an expert with 38 years' experience in the field of insurance claims handling. Terry Hallett FCILA ACCII MIM worked for many years as a Chartered Loss Adjuster for an international company. He has also served as President of his local Insurance Institute.

176pp. illus. 1 85703 317 5.

DEALING WITH YOUR BANK
How to assert yourself as a paying customer

Brian Cain

This book explains in a practical way what your rights are, from managing your current account to obtaining a business loan. Chapters describing popular financial products and how to obtain professional advice will help you cope with managing your money and planning a brighter financial future. Brian Cain is a solicitor and has been actively involved in advising customers of banks. building societies and other organisations for over twelve years.

144pp. illus. 1 85703 379 5.

INVESTING IN STOCKS & SHARES
A step-by-step guide to increasing your wealth as a personal investor

Dr John White

This book has been specially prepared to help and guide those with a lump sum or surplus income to invest, and who are considering investing in quoted securities. This latest edition has been thoroughly revised and updated to reflect the latest developments in the stock market. Dr John White is himself an experienced investor and adviser to an investment company. 'User-friendly ... Contains many practical examples and illustrations of typical share-dealing documents. There are also case studies which give you a feel for your own inclinations about risk versus profit ... Demystifies the world of stocks and shares.' *Own Base.* 'Will be a help to private investors ... Gives an easy to understand guide to the way the stockmarket works, and how the investor should go about setting up a suitable investment strategy.' *What Investment.*

224pp. illus. 1 85703 472 4. 4th edition.

MANAGING YOUR PERSONAL FINANCES
How to achieve your own financial security, wealth and independence

John Claxton

Life for most people has become increasingly troubled by financial worries, both at home and at work, whilst the once dependable welfare state is shrinking. This book, now revised and updated, will help you to prepare a strategy towards creating your own financial independence. Find out in simple language: how to avoid debt, how to prepare for possible incapacity or redundancy, and how to finance your retirement, including care in old age. Discover how to acquire new financial skills, increase your income, reduce outgoings, and prepare to survive in a more self-reliant world. John Claxton is a Chartered Management Accountant and Chartered Secretary. He teaches personal money management in adult education.

160pp. illus. 1 85703 471 6. 3rd edition.

SAVING & INVESTING
How to achieve financial security and make your money grow

John Whiteley

How do you decide what to do with your money? How can you evaluate the risk element? Anyone can manage their own savings and investments; provided that they bear in mind certain straightforward principles. There does not have to be any mystique about saving and investing.' Author John Whiteley is an experienced, practising Chartered Accountant. His work brings him into contact with people from all walks of life.' He draws on this experience to bring to light some simple guidelines that will enable you to decide your own financial goals and priorities, make your own plans, manage your investments, and monitor the results.

144pp. illus. 1 85703 289 6.

PAYING LESS TAX
How to keep more of your money for saving or investing

John Whiteley

For most people tax is a fact of life. You are taxed when you earn money, and when you spend it. You are taxed when in business, and even when you die. This book will show you how to reduce your tax burden – by taking advantage of allowances, reliefs and exemptions, and knowing how to avoid the pitfalls and penalties. You will also learn how timing your transactions can help. Some methods are elementary (though surprisingly neglected), some are a little more complex, but all are explained clearly in this book. John Whiteley FCA is a practising Chartered Accountant. Here he uses many years experience of advising taxpayers from all walks of life, to help you keep more of your hard earned money.

144pp. illus. 1 85703 368 X.

SECURING A REWARDING RETIREMENT
How to really understand pensions and prepare successfully for your retirement

Norman Toulson

In today's changing financial atmosphere, preparing adequately for retirement has never been more important. This extremely useful handbook pinpoints the sources available and the opportunities they offer to suit your circumstances. Whether you are early in your career, about to make a voluntary or enforced job change or nearing retirement, this book will help you plan a financially secure future.

144pp. illus. 1 85703 286 1.